An Essex Education

The working class logic for Brexit. Why we voted for Brexit and ideas for a better UK

By

Mark le-Hope

Brexit, without doubt, has been the most divisive political issue within the UK for a lifetime. And, as the gift that keeps on giving, the failure to implement any coherent strategy on leaving the EU has caused the wounds of the original vote to fester and sore.

As a leave voter I am not joyous or celebratory about Brexit. No divorce is a cause for celebration and the UK finds itself in a sad position of leaving the family home with no plan, no purpose and nowhere to go. That doesn't mean the future will not be a success for the UK, but clearly Brexit cannot be considered as the victorious culmination of a coherent plan or strategy beyond the act of leaving itself.

How did we find ourselves in this position? Does Brexit represent a failure of the EU, the UK or something else altogether?

As a member of the working class being demonised in some quarters for the Brexit vote, I wanted to write this book to try to articulate the logic behind the leave vote. Is it as simple to explain away as the emotive pull of populism, xenophobia within parts of UK society, or does it require a deeper understanding of the challenges faced by many in the UK?

For me, too much of the narrative surrounding Brexit has polarised the personas of the electorate into two clear and distinct characters:

- Remain – the liberal and educated
- Leave – uneducated bigots

1

This doesn't help to properly understand the causes of Brexit, and risks creating further schism at a time when a common strategy and purpose is required. That's not to dismiss the position of those who wish for the UK to remain in the EU and ask them to jump on board the good ship Britannia as it sails into the sunset seeking free trade deals, but it does ask both sides to demonstrate a level of empathy towards the position of those who voted differently. To move forward we need to ensure the causes of the vote are properly understood, irrespective of whether they are agreed with. There is no opportunity to move forward as a nation if the concerns, whether real, imagined or misdirected at the EU, are not addressed.

As a working class leave voter from Grays in Essex I want to outline the reasons for the leave vote as I understand them. Obviously I can't speak for all the people of Thurrock (the constituency) or Essex (72.3% voted to leave in Thurrock and 62.3% across the county of Essex) but I want to record the logic of the arguments for leaving, and frustrations with the EU, that have been shared with me.

An important point to make at this stage of the article is that it is almost entirely anecdotal. No formal research beyond lived experience goes into this text. Therefore a lot of the argument will relate to the perception and emotion of a subject, as much as the reality of it.

Brexit vs. the Brexit deal (the deal for the UK's departure after triggering Article 50)

As I write this the negotiating position of the UK appears to be weak, reflecting a divided government and a divided country. This suggests that the UK may end up with a poor outcome which sees us with no trade deal, potentially leading to a significant economic loss, or tied to EU institutions representing a significant loss of influence compared to the UK's previous position as a full member of the EU. Neither scenario is ideal for either side of the Brexit debate, which reflects the tremendous challenges of departure from a supranational organisation we have been part of for several generations. However, that should not allow the debate over the process of Brexit to be conflated with the debate over the arguments concerning the vote to leave. The two are very distinct and separate.

The more fanciful leaver scenarios would have had the UK sitting in a better position than it occupied within the EU by having free trade with both the EU and the rest of the world, whilst eliminating payments to the EU and discarding common obligations such as freedom of movement. This was never achievable, but the referendum question to leave was never positioned in terms of 'leave the EU and this is what you'll get', in exactly the same way that the remain vote had no explanation for the future of Britain's membership of the EU beyond 'leave the EU and this is what you'll lose'. Fortunately or unfortunately no grandiose statements of the future were included on the referendum ballot forms. Whilst both sides will argue supporters of the other made inaccurate claims, the votes of 35 million people were not decided by messages on the side of a bus. The failure to create any form of consensus post the referendum demonstrates decisions were based on longstanding issues and entrenched world views, and not whims based on flimsy uncosted arguments.

The intention of this book is to focus on the logic of the vote to leave amongst the working classes, but that needs some consideration. The 'working class' is an amorphous mass – it represents the largest socio-economic element of the UK population, so it cannot be viewed as an entity with a single position on any subject. One of the dangers of modern politics is that positions on any subject are being reduced to the binary of 'Yes' or 'No', and lose nuance. This may represent the need of the headline makers to create the appearance of more extreme positions, or it may represent the need of those on social media to grab attention. It is unreasonable to represent the views of such a diverse social grouping as if they are homogenous. Therefore what I will consider are the oft-repeated arguments for leaving.

By way of example – as Scotland and Northern Ireland both voted to remain, and the 'working class' is the largest social group in both countries – the British working class themselves are split on whether to leave or remain given the narrow victory for leave.

Future vision of the EU

An interesting place to start is less the view of the leave voters, and more the arguments from the remain camp. Whilst leave had a clear objective – leave the EU – the remain camp was muddled in its objective. I say this because 'remain in the EU' offered no vision of the future. The effective argument was 'here's what you could lose' which is logical for somebody seeking to maintain the status quo. There are two problems with this argument.

1. It doesn't help you with those who feel they have relatively little to lose. Whether it is the fault of the EU or not, there are millions of people throughout the UK who are seeking change. The British working class has seen their relative wealth decline against virtually everybody else in society as the rich have got horribly rich and the asset owning class below them have seen their wealth expanded primarily through property and share ownership rather than hard work. If the British working classes have seen their relative wealth position decline and recognise that the trajectory is going to continue, the argument of losing the benefits of the existing system doesn't compete against the admittedly more nebulous feeling of hope that change brings. Rip it up and start again. Whether the EU is to blame or not is part of the consideration, and for many the economics of mass immigration are perceived as being a factor in this decline, but the main focus is that it presents an opportunity to vote for change. Whether Brexit will correct the path of the trajectory is a different matter, and again one that needs further investigation, but for too many in society the risk vs. reward consideration of status quo vs. change is balanced in

favour of 'nothing to lose'. Brexit is the change candidate, and those facing a declining position want to enact change. For many leave voters remain vs. leave was effectively stick or twist. For all of the logical arguments about the economic risk to the UK, our society has left too many in a position that they are prepared to roll the dice on a risky future as opposed to a known deteriorating future.

2. The status quo is not the endgame of the EU. If you voted remain you weren't voting for the model of the EU that existed on referendum day 2016. You are voting for a model of the EU that is going to entail closer co-operation and singularity – in both economics and politics. Nobody in the remain camp offered a vision of the future of the EU nor of Britain's role within it. Ask people in Germany, France, Italy, The Netherlands etc. and there is a clear vision of the future of the EU. It is of the EU as a single entity, with a single economy, single jurisdiction and a single political system. I don't recall anybody within the remain camp arguing for that future vision. All of the remain camp arguments related to the economic risks of leaving – arguing for the status quo – nobody offered an argument for further integration or 'more Europe'. It's fascinating that in an argument over the strengths and weaknesses of an institution that nobody arguing in favour of continued membership was prepared to discuss its future goals and the ramifications of that. If the EU's supposed supporters can't make the argument in favour of closer integration, then it is obvious that even those within Britain who voted remain are not publicly comfortable with supporting further integration of the EU.

This sums up one of the great problems of the UK's relationship with the EU – there is no buy-in to a future vision. Even during the midst of the ultimate debate on the value of EU membership, the only argument put forward by remain was economic, positioning the EU as it is, not what it seeks to be.

To provide balance to this discussion I am prepared to argue for the EU despite being a leave voter myself. The 21st century is likely to see the rise of significant political, economic and environmental challenges to Europe from established and developing powers. In the economic sphere the rise of China and India pose a threat, alongside obvious security concerns from Russia and the Middle East. Can Europe continue to rely upon future US military support? How will Europe deal with environmentally displaced peoples given the effect of climate change?

From an economic perspective Europe is in relative decline against developing economies. Globalisation has seen manufacturing in particular move outside of Europe wherever possible to benefit from lower production costs elsewhere. Even the service industry is under threat with call centres and support networks being offshored to low cost environments such as India and The Philippines. Faced with such future challenges it is prudent to look to join as a combined entity with neighbours with whom you share common principles. Whatever the criticism of the EU it has to be recognised that, for the most part, modern Europeans have an expectation of a welfare state, social justice and political representation as well as a generally liberal cultural environment. Why not roll the wagons tight around that and create a single entity for protection and development?

Alongside the economic benefits of the world's largest single market, the countries of the EU can work together to develop a common foreign and security policy to ensure that our common interests are protected.

I couldn't argue with that in the long term and I am sorry that the UK may not be a part of it. The issue is how do you get to that future point and achieve those benefits. Essentially the question is – where will you be sat during the journey? If you were paying more than anybody else on the bus you would probably expect to have the best seat, particularly if you were paying for some of the other passengers' tickets.

The psyche of the UK towards the purpose of the EU has always differed from that of other members. The UK mind-set has primarily focused upon the economic benefit that membership brings. For most Brits the EU was effectively a free trade area supported by NATO for security. Certainly that was the arguments put forward in the previous referendum of 1975. As a child I remember a lot of people referring to the European Economic Community as the 'Common Market'. The perception amongst most Britain's during the 80s and 90s was that Europe was an economic community with eccentric bolt-ons designed to appease the French (Common Agricultural Policy, European Parliament transfer to Strasbourg etc.).

The point missed by most in Britain was that those driving the European vision always wanted to create a superstate. A European superstate is not necessarily a bad thing, as per my argument above. However, there are ways and means by which you can achieve this. No British politician has ever felt comfortable enough to make this argument to the British electorate. Meanwhile the architects of the European superstate have been continuously pushing for such through tied infrastructure and institutions, the most obvious of which being the Euro. This should not be surprising when one considers the origins of the European Union.

The desire for common institutions in Europe arose after the war, most notably amongst the French. They had been invaded by their neighbour Germany twice in living memory. The destruction wrought was such that it had to be impossible for another war between the two countries to occur again in the future. In contrast to the punitive reparations imposed against the Weimar Republic at Versailles after the First World War, post-war France recognised the need to have common interests and goals. The embryonic EU was born out of the common coal and steel management of the Schuman Plan. The logic, driven by the French, and supported by Germany, Italy, Belgium, the Netherlands and Luxembourg, was that no countries would fight with one another when they had common tied interests. Previous rivals should now be partners. Of course, the countries also had to deal with a backdrop of Soviet aggression and the frontline of the new cold war being fought right on their doorstep. A very real threat sat across continental Europe, indeed through the middle of Germany, and so it was essential that Europe was organised in a way that ensured development and garnered support from the US. The Cold War probably raised the stakes in terms of where post-war Europe had to position itself for the future amongst European leaders of the time. For how long could they rely upon US support? For how long could they withstand Soviet aggression? Perhaps that existential threat raised the long-term ambitions over and above mere economic co-operation, which remained the primary mind-set of the UK.

This brings me to a key issue – there has always been a fundamental difference in the mind-set between Britons and continental Europeans concerning the *raison d'etre* of the EU. For continentals it is peace and security as much as it is economics. For the UK it has predominantly been an economic purpose, loosely combined with a need to find a role post-war resulting from the end of the British Empire. Consider that all of the current twenty-eight EU countries have a living memory of dictatorship, collaboration with or occupation by a foreign power, with the exception of the UK. You can even witness this logic assessing the voting patterns in the Brexit referendum in the UK itself – Northern Ireland, a recent conflict zone, and Scotland, a country where close to half of the citizens want independence from the UK (and may well feel they have been occupied for centuries by another country). Depending upon your politics you could easily make a case that both of those countries have been occupied by a foreign power. It's a mind-set that England and Wales do not share. As much as the UK would never have been victorious without US involvement in the Second World War (and

Hitler's decision to launch Operation Barbarossa against the USSR), the UK had fought to repel the Axis powers on its own. The Battle of Britain and the Bletchley code breakers ensured that the UK could survive. This survival instinct, combined with our natural independence caused by being an island nation, and global mind-set from a century of empire, means that we do not instinctively wish to be part of a European superstate. British politicians have never sought to sell us a vision of European integration beyond economics.

Security and survival is a core driving instinct of humankind and it is possible it has consciously or sub-consciously guided other European countries through their internal political obstacles towards closer integration. Such consideration has never been part of the European debate within Britain. The vision of a single European superstate has not been embraced by the British. That is why Britain has always been such a reluctant partner to the European project. At every stage of closer European integration Britain's politicians, of all hues, have failed to address the issue of Britain's long-term position vis-à-vis Europe. I assume that had anybody raised the prospect of a single European superstate in the past the issue of an in-out referendum would also have been raised. Until the arrival of UKIP that was an issue that every British politician had sought to avoid – knowing there was a real risk of a Brexit type scenario occurring. Perhaps had somebody been brave enough to raise it a two-speed Europe could have been a solution at the time of previous treaties without the need for the chaotic uncoupling of Brexit.

No major British politician has come out in favour of Britain as part of a Federal superstate. The remain campaign did not make the case for a European superstate during the referendum. They continued to focus on economics rather than the long-term strategic need for a European superstate. Nobody loves economics. It's not a flag you can wear. It's particularly hard to sell to people who feel they have little of the supposed economic benefits, and what little they do have is reducing.

The remain argument was based on the status quo. 'We don't want to leave because of what we'll lose'. It was a negative argument. It was the opportunity to present their vision for a future Europe and they failed to do so. Even now, when campaigning to block 'no-deal' or champion a new referendum, there is nobody in the UK pushing a vision of the UK within a European superstate.

Leave voters recognise there is no status quo position. The choice in the referendum was – the UK as part of a Federal Europe at some point in the future (Remain) versus an undefined future as an independent country (Leave).

"...we must now face the difficult task of moving towards a single economy, a single political unity." (Romano Prodi, President of EU Commission, 1999)

"The day of the nation state is over." (Roman Herzog, German president, 1996)

Democratic deficit

A big criticism that is regularly thrown at the leave voters is their desire to 'take back control'. It is always delivered with disdain as though control of a nation state by that nation state is a bad thing. Alternatively the criticism must reflect the view amongst many Remainers that Britain always retained control as it had a veto against further integration, thus rendering it a superfluous argument.

If the UK has the opportunity to veto EU developments, then ultimately we have an emergency brake. However, many would not consider that as control. Passengers on a train have the opportunity to press the emergency alarm but they are not in control of the destination or how it is being driven. The reality as perceived by many who voted leave is that the UK has little actual control. The development of the EU is being undertaken behind closed doors by national leaders and the EU Commission, so at best we as UK voters have minor influence in negotiations.

If we are going to argue technicalities, and the veto argument is very much one of technicalities rather than reality, that influence is $1/28^{th}$ if every country has an equal vote and their own veto.

Combine $1/28^{th}$ influence with the fact that the direction of progress is driven by the European Commission who are developing a European superstate. Indeed, it would be like turkeys voting for Christmas if the Commission were to suggest the future EU strategy should be 'Less Europe'. So

Britain's influence is 1/28th of a group who primarily have an agreed purpose of a future European vision that is different to the view of most of the UK. That is not control.

As seen time and again with the development of the European Union, when individual populations have been allowed to vote in referendums they have voted against closer European Union, and yet the outcome has always been that vote has been re-engineered to deliver the 'correct' result (Denmark on the Maastricht Treaty, Ireland on the Nice Treaty and Ireland again on the Lisbon Treaty). Indeed Brexit seems to be going the same way with weak negotiations being led by an admitted Remainer in Theresa May, or a reformed Remainer in Boris Johnson. We've had the referendum and both the EU and the UK politicians are doing their damndest to make us vote again.

"If it's a Yes we will say 'on we go', and if it's a No we will say 'we continue'." (Jean-Claude Juncker)

Some will argue that this reflects minor problems which have needed to be refined within the proposals to get them to be progressed. Others will view it as an example of how the rights of individual people, and even states, are being overridden at the expense of the European project. In much the same way that history is reckoned to be written by the victor, the explanations as to why the Danes and Irish suggest only small amendments were required seem fanciful. Because every voter focuses on the small details of a treaty, don't they? I doubt most of the politicians read them let alone the voters.

"Let's be clear about this. The rejection of the constitution was a mistake that will have to be corrected." (Valéry Giscard d'Estaing)

In the debate over the terms of the Brexit negotiation lots of Remainers have used the analogy of a golf club or members club when explaining the EU's position to reject Britain's requests – for example: 'you wouldn't expect to retain rights to membership if you don't pay the fees or follow the rules'. Indeed, and that logic is understood, but similarly you wouldn't stay in a golf club where you had a fundamental difference over the development and strategy of that club.

For example: 'I don't think we need to enlarge the club because things are good as they are. Let's enjoy playing golf'. 'No, we need more members because it will enable us to have more income to develop a social club'. Outvoted.

'I don't see the need to employ a manager and full-time staff – we've been managing perfectly well as a members committee'. 'Yes, but they will have the time to consider ways in which we can really develop the golf club to reach its full potential'. Outvoted.

'I really don't think we need to be spending time at one another's houses. We enjoy each other's company playing golf, let's keep it like that'. 'No, we need to spend time at one another's houses so that we develop strong bonds aside from golf. That will enable us to grow into an expanded sports and social club and develop a common strategy on all areas of life other than golf'. Outvoted.

'People seem to be coming in who aren't even members or paying fees.' 'Yeah, we noticed that as well, but some of our members keep leaving the fire escape open and say that they don't have enough money to fix the burglar alarm'. Outvoted.

The UK is swimming against the tide, and in needing to maintain some of its own interests, i.e. (rightly or wrongly) financial rights for The City within the single market, successive UK Governments have gone along with structural EU development treaties such as Maastricht because that reflects the horse trading reality of politics. However, being a member of a club is not the same as having control.

The worst thing about all of this is that it is so far removed from the ordinary voter. If you consider the UK political system of elections, the government rarely obtains a majority of the vote. So, a party that represents less than 50% of the population is doing behind closed door deals where it has 1/28th influence. That is not control.

This is compounded when you view it through the prism of who actually finances the EU, given the UK is the second largest net contributor behind Germany, so coming back to the widely used golf analogy, you get the same voting rights as people who are taking from the club's coffers whilst you are financing it. And the real slap in the face is that you are constantly outpositioned in negotiations and told to go with what the majority want.

Another factor that irks many Britons is the perception of European rules never working to our advantage, either as

Britain compared to other countries or as law-abiding citizens compared to law-breakers.

An obvious starting point is the laughable situation of the parliament having to move, at great cost to the taxpayer, between Brussels and Strasbourg. Who does this benefit other than France? There is no logic for it and is typical of the lack of common sense applied to the design of the EU. It infuriates ordinary people who are struggling with austerity and reductions in relative wealth whilst the EU is demonstrating continuous largesse. As a leave voter it is indicative of how the EU project has no respect for the ordinary voter, and perceives itself to be correct, even when sat against the laws of common sense. If this exists now, whilst we are still able to leave, imagine the absurdities once we are properly tied in.

Look at our public services being continuously cut to balance the books whilst the EU just spends with abandon without providing any increase in living standards for the average Briton. Again, when considering this from a perspective of a net contributor, it is highly offensive to the sensibilities of right and wrong.

Perhaps the worst example of the frivolous institutions of the EU is the Common Agricultural Policy. This is a policy set up to benefit French farmers which costs billions and results in farmers overproducing unnecessary product that is unused and wasted simply to secure agricultural subsidies. All the while there are people starving around the world and Britons have to pay more for imported foods due to tariffs on the products that we actually wish to consume.

It should always be remembered, when considering the history of the EU and the UK, that in 1963 and 1967 De Gaulle twice deliberately vetoed UK membership until such time that institutions were established that would favour France over the UK within the EU – notably the Common Agricultural Policy, Common Fisheries Policy, and the way the budget was set.

Immigration

As mentioned at the start of the text the leave voter has been characterised as a swivel eyed racist. There is a massive misconception that any debate regarding immigration also entails issues of race. It does not. The immigration debate is one of numbers, resources and quality of life. Such a debate can be held completely independently of issues of race. Any debate on race incorporates complex issues, but it is not appropriate to conflate issues of immigration with issues of race to frustrate the discussion on immigration. The failure to recognise valid concerns regarding uncontrolled immigration and continually shout down the debate with accusations of racism has undoubtedly played a factor in the vote to leave.

For decades politicians of all parties have refused to address any issues of concern regarding the negative effects of immigration. It is inconceivable that the entry of millions of people into the country doesn't come with negative effects as well as positive benefits. The benefits vs. the negatives of immigration will always be debated and there are many different perspectives to consider – the economic benefits, the cultural benefits etc. However, rather than seek to enter into such a debate the political classes have sought to shut it down by characterising any persons who have voiced concerns over immigration as being racist (remember Gordon Brown on the campaign trail referring to a lady as a bigot without any attempt to debate her concerns). There has been a complete failure to address the topic and this has resulted in understandable frustrations when valid concerns are not being considered for debate.

When considering Brexit the view from many in the remain campaign has been that people's concerns have been demonstrative of the UK working class being racists.

As a member of the working class I can assure you that we are not racists. I believe that the British working class must be one of the best examples of a tolerant and welcoming working class in the world. Look at the amount of mixed race families amongst our working class. There has never been any major political party of note within the UK advocating racist policies. This is different to other major countries of the EU such as Germany, France and the Netherlands.

I am not a supporter of UKIP but I find it frustrating whenever the accusation of racism was thrown at them. I can see no evidence of racism in their policies and I know that they had members from all ethnic backgrounds within their membership. From my perspective the concern raised by leave voters was always one of numbers. It is not practical for any society to have no control over the number of people in its country. How can you make strategic decisions when you have no understanding of the current population, let alone future population?

The quality of life in the UK has been adversely affected by the number of people who have come to the country in recent years. That doesn't mean the people are not good people or have not brought benefits to this country. What it does mean however, is that EU migrants, particularly from Eastern Europe, were not planned for. This has been admitted as fact by Labour. Education, housing, healthcare, public transport, road networks – all of our strategic policies are playing catch up against a net population growth of 300k + per annum. How do you deal with that? This has an inevitable knock-on effect on all areas of normal people's lives. In all of these areas the ordinary person's quality of life has been impacted. This view may have been inelegantly represented as being 'Too many foreigners' (which is not a racist view anyway as it provides no sense of superiority of one race over another), but in reality was a cry of – 'uncontrolled immigration has brought unplanned for challenges to our society which is being most keenly felt by our working classes when they try to access support services'.

I do not understand why the remain campaign accept no link between millions of new people and challenges in education, housing, healthcare, public transport, etc. Where do they think these people are going if not competing with the existing population for these already stretched resources? Do they think that all of these immigrants are working as builders delivering hundreds of thousands of new homes for them to live in, and teachers teaching all of their children, and healthcare professionals providing all of their healthcare?

It is hilarious that you will see well-to-do communities in remain voting areas campaigning against developments in their back yard because of the impact to countryside, green space and infrastructure and yet no question of why these houses are needed in the first place. 'I can't abide those awful leave voters. Why can't they understand that we're all just people? The working class are so ghastly and racists. Not like us. We don't generalise against groups. Right – back to the meeting –

how do we stop this awful development?' The only conclusion is that such people are so insulated from real life that they don't realise there is a problem, or worse, they just don't care, as long as they can carry on virtue signalling on social media.

There is obviously a criticism to be made to the British Governments of the 21st century regarding austerity and underfunding of public services, but I would refer you back to my earlier point – if immigration is not controlled how are the government expected to plan for 300k + persons? They are always playing catch up. It's argued by the remain campaign that immigrants pay taxes too and I completely accept that. However, it has to be recognised that to be a net contributor to the coffers of the state you are reckoned to need to be earning at least GBP 30,000 per annum. How many EU migrants are earning that kind of money? Think of the logistical challenges that brings. I doubt many of the indigenous population are earning north of 30k, let alone migrants who have come to the country without a professional level job. And their families.

I have a friend who married a Polish girl. She is an only child. She is not a net contributor to the state from a tax perspective but she is a lovely person and I wish her all the happiness in the world. As she is an only child her mother is planning on coming to the UK for her old age. She doesn't want to be too distant from her family. She is going to come here once she retires. So, having received absolutely no tax income from this lady, the NHS will have an obligation to provide her healthcare. This is a story that's personal to me, but it can be extrapolated across hundreds of thousands of other people. Per year!

On a personal level, the micro level, there is no anti-EU racism. People are not being attacked because of their race or their nationality. Britain has been a fantastic home to millions of foreigners, both from the EU and beyond. But, on an aggregated macro level, it is madness to have uncontrolled immigration. Why would any country in the world operate a policy whereby you hoover up other countries' OAPs? Why would you operate an open door policy for other countries' unskilled/unprofessional labour?

Uncontrolled immigration is unsustainable. Immigration is only sustainable if you are running a planned immigration policy whereby you only allow in those people who have skills and qualifications that meet a country's specific labour shortages and lack of expertise. It should be a requirement, where possible, that those skills are passed on to the existing population, and you make any offer of immigration linked to a job that ensures net contribution to the UK funds and for a limited period of time. You do not offer citizenship. Migration should be a process of negotiation – if the terms and conditions that we offer are not enough to make you come, you don't come. It's our gaff – wipe your feet. There have to be terms and conditions of entry. In many senses it should be like a job offer. We want highly skilled, motivated people who are keen to embrace our way of life for a limited period and then return home. It's a fixed term lifestyle. If you want to stay longer once you are in the UK then you follow an established process for doing so which requires that a) You are needed at the end of your originally agreed residence period, and b) you are financially able to support yourself.

I appreciate the argument that it is not fair for people to put their lives on hold whilst they are working here as they don't know what the future holds, but if they are coming for work then they will have established it is in their financial interest to do so. If they are coming for a cultural experience then hopefully they will make the most of their time here. Any immigration should be understood in those terms – it should never be open ended. I keep seeing remain voters telling me how unfair this position is ('uncaring, inhuman, racist!') and yet I don't see any other developed nation operating anything differently to what I have proposed. You can't just rock up in Canada, the US, Australia, New Zealand, China, Japan etc. and expect to be guaranteed the rights of a citizen. Why should the UK be different? How can it be a moral duty, other than when it comes to genuine refugees, to provide more than a glorified contract of employment?

I fully understand that people will have lives beyond just work. If people fall in love and wish to marry, or remain in the country as part of a relationship there are rules to do that. But it must be understood that all initial immigration should have a cost benefit for the UK. It is madness to operate an immigration policy that supports the inflow of people who present a net financial loss. Whilst a country and a society should be so much more than just a business it is illogical to place an economic burden onto your country, as well as a social burden, if your immigration policy is managed in such an uncontrolled fashion.

We have the laughable situation where Britain is a net contributor to the EU budget, and is also a net contributor in terms of employing EU citizens, housing EU citizens and providing social benefits to EU citizens, to the point that children in Poland, who have never been to the UK are claiming child benefit. Critics may argue it is reciprocal but how many Brits are working in Poland and claiming child benefit to send home to the UK? I'd love to see that comparison.

Another criticism of the leave vote is that we are accused of wanting to kick out immigrants who work here. 'Who will staff the NHS?' 'NHS exodus!' etc. etc. I don't understand why this argument would be applied. Anybody who is skilled and works in the NHS or a similar industry supporting the country will be entitled to apply for their job, and if they meet the criteria required (which surely they would in the medical sector) they stay. Nobody is asking anybody who is employed and a contributor to the economy to leave. Most leave voters believe that it is morally wrong to expect that people who have followed the rules to come to this country should be expected to leave when they have built a life whilst acting in good faith.

Also, it would be fascinating to understand the numbers on this. Is the % of staff working in the NHS from the EU greater or less than the % of the population from the EU? Given the incredibly rapid growth in UK population can we truly understand whether this EU army manning the NHS is simply the amount proportional to the demands the increased EU population has placed on the NHS? Are the NHS workers all cutting edge surgeons or are they cooks and cleaners? Are they specialists or generalists? Are they irreplaceable or easily replaceable? I'm not sure that we properly understand the statistics and I would wager that the people shouting 'but immigration is good for the economy' don't either. Even if it is good – there is no doubt immigration could be better serving the UK if it was planned. We would have the net contributors, and not have to support the net recipients.

Between 1995 and 2011 the fiscal cost of migrants in the UK was at least £115 billion and possibly as much as £160 billion according to a report from the Centre for Research and Analysis of Migration headed by Professor Christian Dustmann at University College, London. The report found that migrants in the UK were a fiscal cost in every year examined – Migrationwatch UK

Another regular criticism of the leave vote, and the British working class, is that we are lazy and dislike foreigners. Irrespective of whether this is accurate or not (it is clearly not) the hypocrisy of those taking that position astounds me. They are making the same sweeping, ignorant, ill-informed comments about the British working class that they are incorrectly accusing us of making against immigrants. It's amazing how childish and name calling people become when they actually have no logical argument. An element of the leave vote was made by people who want to leave the EU to control immigration because EU membership means it is impossible to control it. That in turn has an inevitable impact on the country's resources – diminishing people's quality of life. That somehow translates into – 'The working classes are all uneducated and racist. They just want foreigners to go home'. Which is as ignorant a mind-set as the imagined working class whose character they are demonising.

Will Self famously made the comment that 'not everybody who voted Brexit is a racist but 100% of racists supported Brexit'. OK, so what's your point? It could be argued that not 100% of Muslims are terrorists despite 100% of terrorists being Muslims. Are we accepting sweeping generalisations as part of a grown up debate now? So there are five British racists and they all voted leave as well as 17 million others. What is the value of this statement, even in the ridiculous event it is true? It is this smearing that has been used to stifle debate over immigration for the last twenty years. The effect of such smearing has not been to create a better, more integrated society, but a fractured society with more extreme views. The frustration for leavers like myself is so self-evident and obvious. Whether immigration is good or not for society will not be accepted by individuals unless those individuals can see the benefits. If your relative wealth has declined, whilst your quality of life has deteriorated during a period of historically unprecedented immigration, people will likely hold a negative view of immigration. The two factors may be completely unrelated, but nobody has been able to demonstrate this to be the case. Screaming racist in people's faces when they make this link will not change their mind.

Continuing to scream racist at somebody who believes in harm being caused to society is like screaming 'heretic' at a person who doesn't believe in God. You're asking me to believe in something that is unlikely to exist and has never been proved to me, and goes against everything I've ever seen or experienced. You are asking me to have faith in 'the economic benefits', whilst everyone around me is experiencing a worse quality of life than they used to. People will not have faith until they see the benefits with their own eyes.

These issues are accelerating throughout the Western World and are more reflective of economics than they are of racism. When immigration is criticised we would like to see the government or the parties in favour of it (effectively all political parties – I can't think of any who are anti-immigration. Even UKIP is anti-uncontrolled immigration) make a coherent case for it.

There is no desire to see foreigners being banned from entering the UK. In fact, I imagine most leave voters would be thrilled to see an increase in tourists and visitors to the UK. We have a country that we are proud to share.

There is a desire to see a reduction in the number of permanently resident people in the country to relieve some of the pressure on our resources. It is not racist to want to be able to protect core services. Inevitably there is a question of whether the decline in public services reflects a failure of governments to provide adequate funding versus the sudden and dramatic population increase brought by immigration.

A large number of Brexit voters believe that uncontrolled immigration directly correlates to the pressures being felt on our public services. There is nothing racist about this position, and the constant accusation that it is fuels the anger and frustration of people who feel that nobody is listening. The sheer number of immigrants, combined with the lack of a credible far-right party in the UK, demonstrates clearly that the

British are not racist and have no desire to 'kick people out'. I would also argue that your typical racist, in the clichéd minds of the critics of Brexit, is likely to be a white working class National Front supporter – campaigning against BAME peoples. Has there ever been a racist position taken against the people of Eastern Europe who racially are fairly indistinguishable from Western Europeans? I'm not even aware of any common term of abuse. Now, that is nothing to be celebrated, but it does show that those leave voters for whom immigration is a concern are not acting from a racist position. Indeed, it could be argued that there is a greater ethnic similarity between the UK and Eastern Europe, as people of Northern European origins, than with Southern Europe. Again, I can't recall any campaigns to omit any Southern Europeans, despite a higher degree of ethnic difference. There has been no mass immigration of peoples of Southern Europeans because they have not secured the same economic benefits in the UK as the people of Eastern Europe. To paraphrase, it's not racism 'It is economics, stupid!'.

Another key element to consider is why the UK has received such an influx of immigrants from other EU countries. The first reason is political. The Labour Government of Blair and Brown signed the agreement to extend the EU in May 2004 to incorporate the A8 countries of Czech Republic, Estonia, Hungary, Latvia, Lithuania, Poland, Slovakia and Slovenia. Blair and Brown granted the citizens of these new EU ascension countries of Eastern Europe to have full rights of employment in the UK. Other countries, notably Germany and France, prohibited this. As a result the doors were fully open.

Labour have subsequently accepted they misjudged the numbers, but how true is that? Is it possible that Labour spotted the opportunity to gerrymander the population by introducing millions of low paid workers who would be semi-reliant on benefits, and far more inclined to vote Labour? In much the same way that Thatcher believed selling off the family jewels of our nationalised industries and public housing stock would make more people Tory voters in the 80s, did Blair and Brown believe they could create a new societal paradigm favouring Labour? Neither strategy worked for either party and has resulted in significant societal consequences resulting in a divided society and a key cause of Brexit. We can't blame the Eastern Europeans for coming and nobody has. However, there is an inevitable tipping point. A small island with limited resources is always going to suffer an impact on quality of life when the population increases rapidly and suddenly. There are invisible measurements to quality of life which cannot be assessed by GDP. The remain campaign are constantly rolling out figures about how immigration is good for the UK economically (though clearly not agreed with by Migrationwatch UK), and I completely agree that there will be an inevitable economic consequence of leaving the single market, but quality of life cannot be measured in GDP. Net immigration of 330k plus a year is unsustainable. Why is the remain campaign prepared to ignore this?

I can't see a GP within two weeks due to the pressure on the NHS. It never used to be that way. This isn't me saying that the failure to see a GP is as a result of uncontrolled immigration due to the EU. I recognise that it is due to a combination of underfunding and poor management, but ultimately it comes down to the demand on the NHS. Now, you may take the view that the challenge on the NHS is due to an ageing population and immigrants are required to bolster the percentage of the population that provide support and pay taxes etc. This is fine if you have a controlled immigration policy – you let in those who are a net contributor to the economy or those whose skills are required to provide jobs that we cannot fill. The EU doesn't allow us to do this and it is damaging the services that a lot of us hold dear. This isn't to blame the migrants as individuals. I fully recognise that a significant % of EU migrants will be employed and will be paying their taxes. They will be supporting the NHS and other services. But even if they are paying their way, and not everybody is, it still produces questions over the quality of life. This isn't some kind of small minded dig at foreign people. It is a question of numbers, and uncontrolled numbers at that, as 3 million EU migrants need to live somewhere. Whilst I recognise the problems of the housing market are primarily fuelled by economic factors (for example, post-2008 quantitative-easing giving rise to cheap credit looking for a return on investment) there is still the issue of how do you house a rapidly expanding and uncontrolled population? I constantly hear the answer being to build new houses, but that simply erodes the quality of life for the people already living in the location. Whilst I appreciate this is NIMBY-ism of the highest order, my quality of life will suffer when:

a) there are more cars on the roads, creating traffic and parking problems including pollution

b) there are more people on trains as there are no local jobs that can afford the new homes and everybody is having to commute to London or other major cities

c) there are more people overloading the local hospitals and schools

d) there are more houses and flats destroying the local countryside

This is not a judgement on the ethnicity or nationality of the newcomer. It is a pure numbers game. Private developers make money whilst our quality of life reduces. For anybody in any doubt come to Grays, Tilbury, South Ockendon, Purfleet, Chadwell St. Mary. Anywhere in Thurrock. Drive down the A13 and see how we are blighted by constant new builds of dubious quality eroding the conventional borders of our towns. Come and see the industrial chimneys and concrete all the way to Southend punctuated by scrappy plots of green space. It is not just South Essex. North Kent is exactly the same and I have no doubt it will be coming to other areas of the home counties and wider south east shortly unless population is controlled (leave the EU) or society finds a way to spread work beyond the south east. This is such a national emergency that central and local government are prepared to ignore warnings and grant development of new homes on flood plains, simply storing up problems for future generations to deal with.

You can't put a value on space. It is not an issue of race or xenophobia – it is an issue of balance. It is not all about money and that is one of the reasons why people voted to leave the EU despite recognising the inevitable economic consequences. The native Essex communities didn't take well to us cockneys coming to their manor after the war. Was that xenophobia? – it can't have been racism as we were all white English. However, it is clear that they weren't wrong when they anticipated a negative change to their quality of life. Whilst a proud Essex boy, I don't think the concreting over of fields and building of crap new towns provided much benefit to the indigenous population.

Quality of life is an intangible. It is not about wealth or personal gain. I keep being told about how much money is generated by immigrants to the UK. That's great but the sheer weight of number of people in the south east is reducing our overall quality of life. Unless that wealth is effectively distributed it is of no value to me. Similarly, overall wealth may be increasing but if the number of people in the population has increased at a higher rate, the wealth per person has reduced. GDP vs. GNP.

If I pick my dream team of the greatest eleven football players of all time I doubt I'll have the same as anybody else. The same would be true for populations. My dream team would be based on my personal likes and dislikes and would include a lot of non-British people. That would mean removing British people I don't like from the team. How do we remove people we don't like from society? Fortunately society doesn't work like that (or shouldn't) and an immigration policy should be based solely on the skills and benefit that an immigrant can bring to their new country. I've met the most wonderful people of all colours, creeds and nationalities. Some of the worst people I've ever had the misfortune to meet are white, British working class people just like myself. That does not reflect that one ethnicity or culture is better or worse than the other, it is just the law of large numbers and the environments in which I am likely to mix with people.

I have mostly mixed with people similar to myself. Therefore they are going to present the widest pool of candidates to fill my best and worst people. When I meet with immigrants through work it is in a professional environment where everybody brings the best of themselves. It's not in the pubs and clubs of East London and Essex where alcohol and drugs, and limited life opportunities for some, leads to increased aggression and violence.

When I have lived in less salubrious parts of London the risk of crime and violence mostly came from non-white youths. This doesn't reflect anything other than the law of large numbers. The best and worst of that environment were going to be non-white because of the makeup of the population. Those who feel that immigration is a problem believe it is damaging their quality of life.

Another aspect to consider is the sense of place. It is an amorphous concept but if you have moved to an environment you are likely to be far more open to the new. You start as a newcomer so you are open minded and keen to explore new opportunities. There is a general feeling that cities voted remain because they have higher levels of education. An alternative view would be that they have more transient populations who themselves are new to an area. People who expect, and may even want, the excitement of a multinational population. One of the big challenges of uncontrolled EU immigration is that it has brought cultural challenges to communities who are not dynamic. People who do not want change. Those who wanted life to remain as it is. A common phrase I have heard from such communities is 'we didn't vote for this' as though they should have been warned that their tired town was going to be transformed by a sudden influx of East Europeans. Whilst I recognise that life moves on, I think there needs to be more sensitivity to those people and communities who simply wanted to remain as they were.

As a net contributor to the EU, should UK citizens be expected to also act as a home for millions of people from countries who are net beneficiaries, with relatively little control over the immigration of those people?

Most working class towns feature the type of people (massive generalisation alert) who are not seeking fame and fortune. They value close proximity to friends and family and a (relatively) low stress lifestyle achieved through having local work. They accepted that their lives would not be wealthy but would be affordable and be rich in other ways. If you move to London, Birmingham, Manchester, Edinburgh, Glasgow or other major cities you expect a more dynamic lifestyle which includes living alongside people of all nationalities. People in quiet towns throughout the UK, but primarily England, did not expect to be subject to such a fast paced cultural transformation. In many ways it is the speed of the transformation that has caused such concerns, particularly when considering the accompanying challenge to resources.

And it is the sneering response of politicians of all hues that people who don't like that sudden change are racist has given rise to the likes of UKIP and the leave vote. The winners of mass immigration failed to take the people of non-metropolitan Britain with them. Whilst people in cities have enjoyed booming house prices, people in small towns have seen a cultural transformation of their high streets whilst simultaneously seeing a reduction in services, and all the time having their concerns being addressed as racism.

Whilst the rich keep getting richer, ordinary people feel they are losing. Whilst immigrants may be the wrong target for the cause of their financial ills, there is a feeling in many people's minds that they are at least a symptom of a government and system that doesn't care about them. The cry of many Brexit voters is 'fix our problems before you introduce more mouths to feed'.

I understand the Remain response to this is that there will be less money in the public pot to spend on services by leaving the EU. I don't necessarily agree with that, although I do agree that in the short term there is likely to be less money in the overall economy. But why can't post-Brexit bring a greater share of public spending? The overall cake may be reduced but the amount spent on public services may increase as a % of the overall which surpasses the current spend. In the medium to long term we do not know what type of political parties will be in power. There is no reason that because the Tories lead the Brexit negotiations that they will win an election. Churchill was a wartime leader. Nobody wanted him in peacetime. The population may feel that the post-Brexit environment needs to be more balanced towards ordinary people than big business.

This brings me onto another concern of mine. Remainers seem to believe that we will be living in some offshore sweatshop, by virtue of the loss of the single market. So, we as UK citizens will all stand aside whilst our rights are crushed? I don't believe the good people of Canada, Australia or NZ needed membership of the EU to have workers' rights or maternity leave. Why do we? We can keep everything we've got and add anything we want as a society. There is no reason why we have to accept a reduction in rights. If Brexit has taught us anything it is that the British public do believe in political debate and will fight for their quality of life. It might have been recently represented in the growth of UKIP for the Brexit cause, but next time it might well be a party campaigning for a more even distribution of wealth or environmental concerns. We're more passionate than a lot of commentators believed. The British working class is not lazy – it is simply underrepresented in the debate. Let's put that energy, Remainer and Leaver, to good use post-Brexit, to build a fair Britain that we all believe in.

Economics

Leaving the EU will inevitably have economic consequences. You can't expect to leave the world's largest trading bloc and find yourself with the same trade opportunities as previously existed. There will inevitably be bumps in the road and I believe that is understood by the majority of people that I speak with. We do not expect magic trade deals to be secured with the EU or the US, China or anybody else that may be interested. This will have an impact on UK wealth which may, or may not, have an impact upon public spending and the quality of life of your average UK citizen. I've read many critiques of Brexit stating that the leave vote was made by the poorest to make themselves poorer. That implies that a Remain vote would have made them wealthier. In absolute terms we will never know, but in relative terms the poor are getting poorer right now – whilst we are members of the EU. Now, you can blame this on anybody you want, and I do not believe that the EU is the sole target for criticism, but the poorest in UK society are caught in a position of unfair competition with EU citizens.

If an unqualified, uneducated EU citizen wants to try their hand at a career in the UK there is nothing to stop them coming here. There are no checks on whether their qualifications are adequate or whether there are sufficient jobs for their sector. There is not even a consideration on whether there is suitable accommodation or GP services – they just come in completely legally. Because the UK economy is generally more dynamic and fast paced than most EU economies we are always creating new jobs, albeit at the wrong level. There are too many menial jobs, on minimum wage, with limited opportunity for career development. Nonetheless, there are jobs. So, should our EU citizen secure employment in the UK they have the benefit of knowing that every penny they earn has far greater spending power in their home country than our UK citizen. Yes, they are in the UK and will have to meet all of the same immediate contributory costs as their UK compatriot – rent, food, tax, fuel, but they have a plan B that none of the Brits have, as moderate GBP savings are enough to get them on the property ladder in their home country. All the time they are in the UK they are gaining experience in the English language. This sounds arrogant but fluent English will enhance their own career prospects should they return to their home country. Experience working in the UK will enhance their prospects. There is no reciprocal 'value added lifestyle' available in the EU for any working class citizen of the UK.

We do not speak a second language. This isn't due to the accusation of arrogance that is regularly charged against us but one of necessity. What language should we learn? At school we were offered French or German. Both languages are impractical at an international level as they are spoken very limitedly beyond their own countries. I appreciate that there are swathes of North and West Africa that speak French but I imagine their work visa requirements would make Donald Trump blush. Not very practical for any poor Brit seeking a career overseas. What language should the working class Brit learn? Where should they go? Why not learn Danish? – great idea, they make Lego and have a fantastic quality of life. Ten years from now their economy is in the toilet and your Danish language skills are worthless. Not my problem – I learnt Slovenian so I'm in clover. What? Their economy is running behind the UK economy for growth and there are fewer job opportunities there than at home? Damn.

Language is an example of unfair competition. As much as we may want for our youth to move abroad and work, what's the point? Whatever they earn will be worth less than the equivalent in sterling, so all the time they are abroad they will be becoming relatively poorer (this argument could be applied equally to property price growth as well). This, combined with the fact they won't secure work because they won't speak the language, because understandably it's not taught, puts us as a nation at a massive disadvantage. We can't export people. For all of the understandable cries that Brexit has limited our children's future to go and live and work in the EU it really hasn't. If your child's a professional and work wants them to go, then they will still go. If your child isn't a professional, and I'm betting that's a reasonable % of the leave vote, then they were never going anyway.

A Polish kid can gain a value added lifestyle by working in a chip shop in Grays. They are getting upskilled and relatively richer than if they were doing the same unskilled job in their own country. A British kid doing the same in Poland is getting relatively poorer and is gaining a language skill that only operates in one country in the world. It's a skill but there ain't much demand for it. Then, what happens when you want to return to the mother country? You've been priced out by all the immigrants that came the other way.

When considering the loss of freedom of movement from a UK perspective it's a one-way street. We have no realistic ability to go and work in the EU. How many of us ever took up the opportunity? And I don't mean ex-pats working in ex-pat communities. I mean genuinely embracing work and a career in a foreign country. I don't know many people and I work in the City of London amongst people who had the opportunity. We'll lose something precious, I agree, but it was something that was rarely utilised by the working classes. It's like moving out of a flat complex that had a gym. You loved having it there, swore you'd use it one day, but never did, and could never see how you would.

It's a lot like moving out of London. You sell up for a better life in the sticks where there is more space to raise a family etc. You accept you can never go back because you now live in a house with a garden. If you get comfortable in that environment are you ever going to move back to London to live in a box? It is a young person's game and immigration is similar. The young EU citizens coming here can't lose. They speak the language to varying degrees, and they are likely earning far more in real terms than they could earn back home (I fully recognise Brexit has brought closer parity in EUR/GBP terms, but this is the pre-2016 argument, and there are other financial considerations such as housing). The UK can't benefit from that in reverse.

Our professional young will always travel the world and they still will post-Brexit. But what about our ordinary people? What options do the working class have? Of course there will always be wonderful examples of a kid from a council estate who now runs a successful business in Europe, and good luck to them. It's to be applauded, but it's a rare exception where luck and timing will have inevitably played a part. On a macro level it doesn't work for us. What's the point earning minimum wage in Romania? You are still working class, but now you're living that lifestyle in Romania. You are just as relatively poor as if you're on minimum wage in the UK yet you can't do anything practical with anything that you save. Even if you are lucky enough to develop a professional career in Romania and start earning real local money, it's still worth next to nothing if you wish to move back home. Five years savings of 10% of salary in Romania versus five years savings of 10% of salary in UK. It's not reciprocal. If it's not reciprocal it's not fair. Of course 'freedom of movement' is reciprocal in law, but in practice it's impossible to achieve. We are supporting the young, unemployed workers of the EU who are benefitting from unfair competition – they have a lower cost base.

This is no different to internal migration, but it feels a lot less unfair when you know it is part of a closed circuit, and part of a societal plan that can be influenced by government policy. If people were goods, at the level of unfair competition brought by East European accession, there would be tariffs and anti-dumping duties imposed.

What is particularly unfair about the EU migration situation is that it will never end. As long as the UK is producing more jobs than other countries they will keep coming. Look at our quality of life – a dark, grey, congested, cold, wet landscape. And still they come.

No chance of a job in your home country – go to the UK. What do we say to our young? Try Dublin? Maybe, but it's very expensive as well. Where else do we suggest? This means that the UK, Germany and a handful of other countries are supporting the young and unemployed of other countries. This brings me on to the issue of competition. It's not a case of 'they took our jobs' but it is definitely a case of 'a massive increase in population has created a situation where employers have the whip hand when it comes to unskilled and moderately skilled labour'. This of course has led to a situation where a massive increase in population fuels a housing costs boom whilst simultaneously suppressing wages. A massive increase in population = under supply of property. A massive increase in population = oversupply of labour. And yet people keep telling me that none of these issues are to do with the EU. EU freedom of movement makes both of these situations possible. Indeed, not only possible, but permanent. The lack of ability to plan for population increase has resulted in a perfect storm for non-professional Brits. Increased costs of living combined with stagnating wages combined with increasing competition for social services = reduced quality of life.

There is no way to change this dynamic whilst we are in the EU. Had the EU sought to understand the frustrations within the UK they would have understood that they were reasonable and justified. When Cameron approached them prior to the referendum they should have sought to agree practical limits. Freedom of movement guarantee should be for limited numbers of people between states to ensure balance and reciprocity. This is something that could be explained to the UK electorate.

Forgive the chancer in me but here is what the UK should have done with the EU:

Retirees shipped to new estates in the cheapest towns in Romania and Bulgaria. Why bring the workers to the UK when we can take the patients to the EU?

Want your pension to go further – live in Poland.

Unemployed and costing the taxpayer a fortune in housing benefit – UK council estates built in Slovakia.

We would have created enclaves of the UK throughout Europe and would have massively reduced the spend for the same service in the UK.

The local economy in those countries would have benefited from increased local jobs and spending whilst the UK benefits from significantly lower costs. A friend of mine had to pay for a carer for his father-in-law in Poland. A carer would visit once a day for thirty minutes. The cost? Fifty pounds a month!

In such a scenario we could say – right – you can have as many Romanians in the UK as we have UK citizens in Romania and no more. Make it balanced. Then it seems fair to those who feel they are being affected.

Unfortunately those at the head of the EU institutions are more interested in their own personal legacy than the quality of life issues of their citizens. They are looking to create a superstate and do not care how they get there.

'I have never understood why public opinion about European ideas should be taken into account.' (Raymonde Barre, French Prime Minister and Commissioner)

'The "no" votes were a demand for more Europe, not less.' (Romano Prodi, former President of the European Commission)

Brexit could have been avoided by selling the long-term vision of a United Europe, and accepting that there were numerous routes on how to get there. Instead the British have been lent on as one of the major net contributors to the EU budget combined with being one of the major employers of internal EU migrants. Irrespective of the economic gains to the UK economy, if they are not equally shared out, there is a negative impact upon the quality of life of the average UK citizen. Even if the economic benefits of migration were spread evenly across the UK what would it actually result in – more expensive houses and assets. People would have more money to spend on property, which is limited by virtue of the sheer weight of uncontrolled immigration. No matter how you spread the wealth, those with more get richer. It's Monopoly played out in real life. No matter where you land you are putting your hard earned cash into somebody's pocket who is not actually earning income but extrapolating wealth. It's not the EU's fault in isolation, it is capitalist society, and the criminal numbers of non-EU migrants where governments have had control reflects that. Nonetheless, freedom of

45

movement clearly exacerbates the problem and is a fundamental reason in the vote for leave.

On a macro level controlled immigration can be good, particularly if undertaken to enhance the quality of life of the indigenous population and not solely for the interests of business. On a macro level uncontrolled immigration can never be good. It simply pushes the indigenous population into competition with the immigrants. In extreme scenarios this can result in conflict. In most scenarios this results in a deterioration of quality of life as more people compete over limited resources. The Bank of England themselves** (keen supporters of remain if you recall Mark Carney's horror predictions) have confirmed that recent immigration to the UK has suppressed the wages of the British working class. How can it not? Irrespective of your views on economic policy nobody can argue with the truth of demand and supply. A massive influx of low skilled labour will have an effect on the ability of all unskilled labour to secure better pay. Would we really have had to witness the wide scale introduction of zero hours contracts had there not been uncontrolled EU immigration providing a limitless stream of people to the UK? With a limited pool of UK workers this would never have been accepted. However, for the reasons I outlined earlier regarding the unfair economic advantage brought by an immigrant, the UK workers have been undercut and effectively their rights reduced. This despite the remain campaign constantly telling us that only the EU can protect workers' rights. Thanks for the protection! What's the point of increased rights at work if there is less work and less quality work? i.e. – Julia no longer has her ass pinched at work because of a) EU laws, or b) because she can't find any work that pays the rent, meaning she no longer works.

Staff Working Paper No. 574 The impact of immigration on occupational wages: evidence from Britain Stephen Nickell and Jumana Saleheen

http://www.bankofengland.co.uk/research/Documents/working papers/2015/swp574.pdf

Remainers regularly make the point that Britain makes back enormous times more in trade than the contributions paid by the UK Government. That may be true, but the two are not an exact or fair trade. The UK's contributions are paid through UK Government funds. If not sent to Europe these funds could be used for public services. Whilst the amount of money provided to the EU can come back tenfold or a hundred fold in trade, how will it be distributed? It will be a benefit retained in the pockets of the wealthy – those at the top of society already. It is of no benefit to the working class.

In response you could argue, yes, but trade does provide jobs and employment – and companies have to pay tax on profits, so it all benefits the UK. That is not an unreasonable position if we are arguing on a GDP basis. The UK economy, as a whole, may benefit from EU membership, and this may well outweigh the membership contributions from the UK. Nonetheless, when considering on an individual basis it presents an enormous challenge for the members of the working class. The

47

jobs that are created have been low level jobs requiring few barriers to entry. Such jobs are of course open to any EU citizen, who are now in direct competition with the UK citizen.

On top of this you have the deeply unpleasant situations where, whilst trade may exist in the UK, companies are able to offshore their tax contributions to other EU countries who operate a lower level of tax. You can operate in the UK, using non-British EU labour, who may well be subsidised by the taxpayer through in work tax credits, whilst declaring all of your corporate profits in Ireland or the Netherlands who charge lower corporation tax, variations of which are termed the 'Double Irish', or 'Double Irish with a Dutch sandwich'. The business reaps the benefit of the UK whilst providing very little back to it. So any benefits of freedom of movement, for companies and people, result in the effective privatisation of UK tax spend whilst providing no social benefits. The sheer contrast in numbers between EU migrants to the UK and UK migrants to the EU demonstrates this.

The majority of UK migrants to the EU are retirees who are not competing with the domestic population for work. Their earnings are provided through pensions. There may well be an element of competition for housing (as per the same argument in the UK), but as retirees they will not be competing in areas close to jobs, unlike economic migrants to the UK. Similarly, because they are not in work they are not being provided with in work tax credits or other benefits from the host nation. There could be an argument about healthcare, and that may be greater for retirees, but retirees don't have children or education costs or benefits to be financed.

It would be great to see as part of any debate on the EU exactly what number of Brits live in EU versus EU citizens in the UK. Then strip that down to understand the social costs. Who are net beneficiaries and who are net earners? I can't imagine there are many homeless UK citizens in the EU, yet there are thousands of EU homeless in the UK. I can't imagine there are many UK citizens claiming unemployment benefit in the EU, yet there are thousands of EU claiming benefits in the UK. How many UK criminals in the EU versus how many EU criminals in the UK? How many UK citizens utilise the equivalent of 'right to buy' or other government subsidies to buy homes in the EU? How many EU citizens have utilised right to buy in the UK, aiding profits for private companies at the expense of the taxpayer. Why do we never get these figures? This would help to make us understand the economic argument.

At the bottom of a road I used to live on there are two big new distribution centres of a web based retailer. A lot of the staff there are non-UK citizens. I do not know whether this internet site pay enough to require their staff not to have to claim in work benefits, but let's assume some do claim. Then there are additional benefits such as child credit. All the time these people are sustaining a company that pays almost zero tax in the UK. Is this the future the working classes have to look forward to? Competing with foreigners for the right to work in a distribution centre who make money off the backs of UK Government subsidies whilst paying all of their profits overseas to avoid paying UK tax, which is inevitably higher to finance the massive influx of foreigners using our social welfare system?

Who actually wins in this situation? Shareholders (maybe British but most are based in the US). Property owners renting out flats and houses to EU workers. These landlords maybe British, but are taking UK subsidised money by way of in work benefits and child credit and putting it in their pockets. Who else wins? OK – there are jobs which will generate an element of income tax, but if you require 30k plus to start being a net contributor I am guessing that 95% plus persons employed on that sight are not giving to the UK pot. Yet they need schools and doctors and roads and emergency services.

Coming back to an earlier plea of leave voters – when does it end? We bigoted, uninformed leave voters need to understand the Remainers logic for how this situation fixes itself whilst we remain part of the EU.

Regional vs. International representation

Another concern of being part of the EU is the reduction in the UK's voice at an international level. This is not meant to be any kind of cry of 'The UK is a world power', but more to reflect that when trade deals and international agreements are negotiated Britain's voice is at a $1/28^{th}$ level. We would be more flexible and able to respond in a fashion that targets the particular strengths and weaknesses of the UK economy out of the EU. By having to cut deals within the EU before even negotiating with an external body, the UK's position is marginalised. This results in particular national champions ('The City') being supported to the detriment of other areas of the UK economy.

As globalisation means more truly international standards and deals being agreed is there any value in the UK limiting itself to a voice within a regional entity such as the EU? Or is it better to have its own voice at the top table? Admittedly the UK will never have the same economic influence as the EU, but surely it is better to have the opportunity to be heard and to attempt to negotiate at the senior level than risk being constantly out positioned within a regional group that is then responsible for representing your interests.

Can the UK achieve more by being within the EU or outside? Clearly it will depend upon the circumstances of each issue. For issues of economics the UK will likely secure better trading deals with the US, Japan, China when being part of the EU. However, for matters of societal issues (gay marriage, environmental issues, political reform), are we not better being leaders and influencers on a truly global level than compromisers at a regional level?

The flip side of the argument is obviously that we are stronger as a combined entity and that is recognised, but it does come back to what level of representation you want. If we want our elected representatives to represent us, we need them to speak clearly at the decision making level, not in a behind closed doors deal compromise. How can we judge their successes or failures if everything is horse trading behind closed doors? For all of the obvious flaws of somebody like Trump, at least his voters can see him doing something which can be assessed and judged.

Nobody is to blame for this, it is simply a reflection of how such institutions inevitably create such outcomes. The issue with such a situation is that UK society is skewered towards certain elements of its economy over others. Now, fixing this will not simply require a departure from the EU. It will require decades of government policy to decentralise the economy so that the benefits of the UK finance industry are shared more effectively throughout the UK. However, remaining within the EU means that such a situation will never be addressed. In many ways this sums up all of the issues. Brexit is not the result of an anti-EU agenda by most leave voters. It is a symptom of the malaise of British society, and the repeated failure of generations of politicians to do anything to fix it. For too long Britain's politicians have used the EU as an excuse for inhibiting their ability to enact the change that was promised. If we want to improve our politicians we need to take this crutch away from them.

Ultimately, Brexit represents a cry for the forgotten and for those who can see their future expectations deteriorating. Social mobility is decreasing, debt is increasing. The cost of living is increasing whilst the quality of that life is deteriorating. Why are we paying more for less? This is the same question being asked throughout the Western World. It is not just Brexit.

The reasons are obviously complex, and in the majority of cases they are not solely the fault of the EU. However, the vote for Brexit is a vote for change, and if the politicians and elites don't recognise the need for positive change they will have further shocks like this coming. There is a global fear of 'populism' being on the increase. There is no fear at our level. There is a desire and a demand for it.

Democracy

Another issue that needs to be considered is one of democracy, or a sense of democracy. The EU operates on a system of one state, one vote. Is this fair to the UK? That means that individual citizens of small countries have far more representation at decision making level than major countries. How can it be fair that a citizen of Malta has twenty times the representation than a citizen of the UK? Particularly given the UK's position as net contributor to the EU pot. We have a bizarre situation where the UK, given its cautious view on future integration, has only one vote despite subsidising other members who also get one vote. That doesn't strike many leave voters as equitable. Yet Remainers are constantly telling us that the EU is a democratic institution.

Similar absurdities apply to seats in the European Parliament. Small countries have multiple times the representation of larger countries. For example, Luxembourg has one MEP per 70k head of population and Malta have approximately one MEP 90k per head of population. Guess what the good old taxpayer of the UK gets? One MEP per almost 900k head of population. So our vote is worth 1/10 of a Maltese voters. Yet we are net contributors. Taking our tax to pay for a parliament in which we have one tenth of the democratic representation of a state who is net beneficiary of our contribution.

So, not only does the UK suffer a cost of membership deficit, we are also asked to experience a democratic deficit when it comes to the EU. As the second largest country by population in the EU, that means that we are disadvantaged in relation to twenty-six other countries. Combine that with the position as a net contributor and it is evident that the EU structures are non-beneficial to the UK.

I can't fathom how people can view Scottish nationalism as some kind of positive political movement, yet British people seeking to take back control from EU are viewed as xenophobes. Surely the Scottish Nationalist movement aim is to take back control from the UK to secure fairer representation and greater control of decision making? That is despite the fact that Scotland is a net economic beneficiary within the Union and has greater political representation per head at Westminster than the UK has at Brussels. It is laughable to criticise leave voters desire to bring back control whilst championing Scottish independence when the Scots actually secure greater benefits from the UK than the UK does from the EU.

If I were Scottish I would vote SNP. Not because I hate the Union but because I would always want representation as close to me as possible. I don't trust the buggers to represent me in Europe – not because I'm anti-European but because I recognise that politicians have their own vested interests. The further away from their populations that they operate, the further away from real life and accountability they are. It is this distance that gives rise to the accusation that politicians operate in a bubble. They do not recognise the electorate as their masters, but their subjects. I appreciate there will always be honest exceptions, but for the last few decades we have seen the rise of the professional political classes who operate solely for their own interests with no identifiable cause.

(Brexit is an obvious cause celebre and bravo to all politicians for actually taking a position, even if it is one I disagree with. It should not be forgotten though that many politicians seem to have run counter to their own personal beliefs for the benefit of their career or party which is frankly reprehensible and should never be forgiven.)

The same logic applies to Brexit. I cannot trust any politician to implement the will of the people without getting embroiled in their own political power play. Therefore, the opaque nature of politics in Brussels means that I am not properly able to assess the performance of my representatives.

This is what people talk about when they say they want to bring back control. Many people feel powerless against the trends of the modern world. The political system seems to offer very little by way of representation to ordinary people. If fundamental decisions are being made by people you can't influence and your country has $1/28^{th}$ of the decision making ability despite your country contributing your badly needed funds you are likely to say enough is enough. That position is compounded further if you didn't even vote for the UK Government of the day. In that case your say at the EU table is effectively nothing.

Whilst we can argue that the UK Government's performance of the day will be judged and influenced back home in elections, it is never high enough up the UK agenda for people to vote accordingly. That is why generations of UK Governments have quietly signed up to treaties on further integration without providing the UK electorate a say. How many of the EU treaties of the past would have come into play had the UK electorate been given a referendum? Perhaps Brexit would never have occurred if we had had our concerns addressed at an earlier stage. A confirmed reluctance for further integration from UK voters would likely have resulted in a two-tier Europe where Britain would have maintained the benefits of the Single Market without the need to exit the EU in whole to resolve a lot of the problems perceived by leave voters in the 2016 vote. Although based on the below, probably not.

'If it's a Yes we will say "on we go", and if it's a No we will say "we continue".' (Jean-Claude Juncker, as President of the European Council)

'They must go on voting until they get it right.' (Jose Manuel Barroso, President of the European Commission)

Is it wrong for people to want the decisions that affect their lives to be made by their own political representatives and not by somebody else's? I don't see how that could be considered bigoted or xenophobic. I can understand why the EU encourages one member one vote because it encourages cautious nations to enter, on the promise that you don't have to further integrate unless you want to. However, to be the lone voice amongst twenty-eight is going to be difficult in any situation, particularly if you have become so reliant on the EU single market.

For those who champion the democracy of the EU consider this for its future position. The Commission – the very unelected bureaucrats that many leavers rail against – have proposed a system for future Governance of the EU called reverse qualified majority voting. In such a scenario all of their proposals would become law unless the Council (the opaque discussions of the representatives of twenty-eight different countries) decides by qualified majority to reject within a given timeline! This is like the UK Civil Service introducing a proposal that would require parliament rejecting it to avoid it becoming law. This is the Remainers hope for the future of EU democracy? Thanks but no thanks. Even if you wish to sneer at the desire to take back control please recognise there is a logic to the position.

'According to the reverse qualified majority voting (RQMV) procedure proposed by the Commission in the context of the economic governance package, a Commission recommendation is deemed to be adopted unless the Council decides by qualified majority to reject the recommendation within a given deadline that starts to run from the adoption of such a recommendation by the Commission.'

europa.eu

A response to remain critiques of Brexit

'All leave voters are racist' – as noted above, the logic for leave reflects a decline in quality of life where mass immigration is perceived as a factor. Mo' people = Mo' problems. Politicians and institutions are too slow to respond. Clearly the blame does not lie with the individual immigrant. To channel 1990s Hip-Hop for a moment – 'don't hate the immigrant, hate uncontrolled immigration'. Too much immigration, at too fast a pace, has caused problems that the working class experience in terms of access to social services, including health and education, as well as an economic situation which works against them because of the basic laws of supply and demand. Supply and demand issues that are compounded because the immigrant has a lower cost base and the benefits of unfair competition.

Please remember this is not a British issue, or a white issue. The same situations exist all over the world. Black South Africans turn against black immigrants from other African countries because they perceive an economic and social challenge. Burmese against the Rohingya. Mexicans against other Latin Americans. It is universal. It is not racism, or xenophobia – it is the perception of an economic threat, and a risk to the quality of life of the indigenous population. If we are wrong prove us so. You will never win a vote arguing for uncontrolled immigration and rightly so, yet that is what both political parties have given us, and that is what remain are effectively advocating.

'The British working class are lazy' – of course we are. Because the majority of the population, and the majority of UK taxpayers are lazy. Please don't confuse the working class with a very small 'underclass' you think you know from gross misrepresentations on Jeremy Kyle – you are showing your own bigoted prejudices and complete lack of understanding of the real world. As outlined above how can the British working class expect to compete with the immigrant who has a lower cost base and is upskilling by virtue of menial work through the development of English language skills? If it helps you to feel better about taking this position I would rather be served in a coffee shop by a smiling immigrant than a hostile British 'Yoof', but I completely get why one is smiling and one ain't. One has a future, one doesn't. One is in an exciting adventure in multinational UK, the other one's life may be limited to this job with very little chance of ever securing a home in the area they grew up in.

'We need immigration to support an ageing population' – almost the same as above. So, Brits won't wipe elderly ass even though we've done it since time began? If caring for the sick and elderly was paid appropriately and supported a reasonable lifestyle (as it did until financial deregulation in the 80s) there would be no need to bring in immigrants. The worst part of this logic is that it is completely unsustainable. So, even if we accept this logic, we now have an influx of millions of twenty-somethings artificially added to the population to support the UK elderly. Great. Who supports the immigrants when they reach pensionable age? Using the logic of this position the answer is – 'more immigrants'. It is the ultimate

Ponzi scheme! Flip the situation on its head and see where it leaves us. An ageing population with a declining population = 'OK, Grandad. I'll get your shopping, but I want the house'. Forgive the extreme example but straight away you've transferred the generational wealth gap. By reducing the population we can see the working classes secure more for their labour. If this is paid for by those with wealth all the better for it. Instead of more and more crappy edge of town developments on flood plains with, hilariously, no parking spaces and no bus services (thanks town planners! Oxymoron if ever there was), we would see the population reduce and be able to access larger properties. Or (again – extreme example, and would require more planning in reality) you swap pensioners in houses with families in flats. A portion of town centre newbuild flats become old folk's homes and families get a suburban house. If humanity is to survive we need to be planning for a managed decline in population – not expanding it. The England water board has just announced that water supplies will not be sustainable in only twenty-five years' time due to climate change and our old friend population growth. Will you believe us then Remainers? Do you really need to be without water before you accept that increased population is creating challenges?

These immigrants can be white, black, brown, yellow, blue – they all need supporting with resources. Unless they are contributing more than the existing population they become net recipients. Without the control of who comes in we risk our society becoming financially weaker, not stronger. If there is no financial benefit to the indigenous population of immigration then what is its value? Even if the new migrants are more economically valuable than the existing population (i.e. net contributors) you still have issues of water and land resources. Coming back to my earlier analogy of a football club – you would just sell on or release those becoming a burden. What do we do with all of our economic burdens? Uncontrolled immigration is just pushing them further and further away from ever having the chance to become a contributor.

'The UK could have stopped immigration if it had applied EU rules' – completely agree. However, the UK Governments have had purposes for not doing so. Both parties in power have made decisions that would suggest they are too closely aligned with the interests of big business. Both want cheap labour, and for Labour the perception that immigrants would be more inclined to require state services and therefore vote Labour. Is it possible that they were deliberately diluting the per capita wealth of the country for political purposes? What other excuse can there be?

Former Labour speech writer Andrew Neather was quoted as saying the aim was to 'rub the right's nose in diversity'. Well done Andrew et al – your attempted gerrymandering of the population has created Brexit. Hope you all sit back and enjoy the fruits of your labour.

'Britain can veto a Federal Europe' – Yes, in theory. But as outlined previously other EU countries seem to have already accepted this is the destination. We haven't had that discussion. Had we have done the vote would have been a rejection such as it is now. Britain needs to leave the EU to want to be part of a Federal Europe. Otherwise this issue will pollute our politics for generations. Being the only member who is against closer integration is not a sustainable position for either the UK or the EU.

It appears that both of the two main British political parties recognise that their parties will be split down the middle on this issue. The FPTP system that has retained both parties' positions for decades can be completely destabilised if there is a pro or anti-EU party in play. It splits the vote.

Look at Thurrock in the last three elections –

2017 General Election: Thurrock

	Votes	%	±
Conservative	19,880	39.5	Increase 5.8%
Labour	19,535	38.8	Increase 6.2%
UKIP	10,112	20.1	Decrease 11.6%
Liberal Democrat	798	1.6	Increase 0.3%

2015 General Election: Thurrock

	Votes	%	±
Conservative	16,692	33.7	Decrease 3.1%
Labour	16,156	32.6	Decrease 4%
UKIP	15,718	31.7	Increase 24.3%
Liberal Democrat	644	1.3	Decrease 9.4%

2010 General Election: Thurrock

	Votes	%	±
Conservative	16,869	36.8	Increase 3.6%
Labour	16,777	36.6	Decrease 9.6%
Liberal Democrat	4,901	10.7	Decrease 0.4%
BNP	3,618	7.9	Increase 2.1%
UKIP	3,390	7.4	Increase 4%

This is why Labour and Corbyn have been so terrified to take a position on Brexit. Look at the effect that the growth of UKIP had on the 2015 election, and then its decline post the referendum. Failure to complete Brexit (or failure to thwart Brexit depending upon the environment) results in a split which cannot be repaired along old party allegiances.

Exceptionalism – The vote to leave reflects a belief in British (or even more sneeringly – English) exceptionalism. I'm not sure where this perception comes from but it seems to imply that somehow leave voters, particularly the English leave voters, perceive themselves to be superior to other nations. I can assure you it is not an argument that has ever been presented to me as a logical position to leave the EU. The British working class have never been privileged enough to experience exceptionalism. Indeed, I would argue the vote to leave comes from the exclusionism, rather than exceptionalism, of the British working class. We are not seeing the benefits of membership that other elements of British society are, nor the benefits that other EU states' working classes are (see car manufacturing plants in Slovakia for example – where JLR agreed to move to in 2015, a year before the referendum, as wages are less and the Slovakian Government are believed to have offered JLR €130m of aid to support construction of the factory). If they are not 'coming here to take our jobs' (forgive me the cliché – it's provided knowingly) they are taking our whole industry!

We know that the name Great Britain is not a reference to an innate superiority of the UK, but rather a differentiator of Britain from Brittany.

Brexit has nothing to do with the war. There is no desire to refight the Second World War. Nobody is anti-German, or anti-European. Are the British working class proud of Britain's victory? Of course, but not for any nationalistic purpose. Rather it was a backs against the wall, 'all in it together' achievement. A victory as one, irrespective of class, against a truly evil enemy in Fascism. This also gave rise to our reward – the NHS, social welfare, greater social mobility. Anybody who sees pride in that achievement as being anti-European, or anti-immigrant, are sorely mistaken. The British working class do not see themselves as better as or worse than anybody else. What we previously expected, and now need, as it has become apparent it has been lost, is for our political leaders to prioritise our needs over the needs of the already wealthy in this country, and foreigners. We simply struggle to understand why prioritising British workers or British interests over foreign interests is a bad thing.

As the second largest contributor of oversees aid globally we query what is wrong with also seeking to improve the lives of our citizens at home, as opposed to what feels like everybody else's. The gains achieved through the post-war consensus – the NHS, social welfare and greater social mobility have been eroded. How do you think we will react? This goes left-wing, or it goes right-wing, but clearly the people can't continue to follow centrists (i.e. professional politicians) who only seem to be interested in maintaining the path for big business and themselves to expand their wealth at the cost of everybody else.

'Rejection of Experts' – supposedly we are all ignoramuses voting on emotion as opposed to rational views espoused by 'the experts' (who coincidentally all happen to be Remainers! Thank the stars). This obviously comes from Michael Gove's quote – 'I think the people in this country have had enough of experts with organisations from acronyms saying that they know what is best and getting it consistently wrong.' Clearly that was a poor deflection tactic when he couldn't debunk an expert opinion. However, nobody I know is going to dispute the experts on matters of fact, e.g. climate change. It's real and it threatens us all. Nobody I know is going to argue against the holocaust – it happened. We all know. Nobody is going to argue with scientists over scientific matters - they are experts. The problem comes when applying the term 'expert' to politics and economics. These are not true sciences. There are no experts. We have seen the repeated promises and lies of politicians fail to deliver on so many occasions we are completely immune to what they say. We know the system has been gamed. We know that politicians are bought or have vested interests. I once voted for a politician who promised, in his manifesto, that there would be no increase in tuition fees. A week after my vote that same politician had joined forces to treble them. We get one vote every five years and that is the best we can hope for?

Brexit is not a rejection of experts – it is a rejection of the political classes, the elites they represent, and the 'bought' experts who represent them. Remember Labour said that only tens of thousands of migrants would come when they opened the doors to Eastern European migration. How can we ever trust experts again? Our country has been destroyed on the back of experts who we know have been bought. The rejection is of the game as much as the individual players. We see government projects costing billions fail – what experts were used? The same experts we are supposed to rely upon for economic forecasts re. Brexit? Remainers seem to believe that because we did not meekly toe the party line we are stupid. Quite clearly the working class is voting for change because the current path is unfavourable to us, and frankly, unsustainable to all.

'Brexit is the manipulation of the uneducated by the wealthy' – of course it is. Because clearly all UK political parties in no way represent the wealthy. Goldman Sachs in no way represent the wealthy. The Bank of England in no way represent the wealthy. *The Times, The Independent, The FT, The Telegraph, The Guardian* in no way represent the wealthy. Yes – my current bedfellows currently include some nasty Tory bastards. I do not feel that their purpose for Brexit is the same as the working class leave vote. I fear Brexit may expose many of the institutions I hold dear, but just because some greedy gits want it to be does not mean it shall come to pass. Churchill won the war in 1945, Labour won the election in 1945. We just want positive change. We are not voting leave to destroy workers' rights, women's rights, employees' rights, religious rights, minority rights, LGBT rights. Most of these rights existed within the UK long before the majority of EU countries. We are an advanced society – the British working class are traditionally Liberal in the truest sense of the word – 'live and let live'. Brexit will not force us backwards on these issues. We will not accept the erosion of them. Rather than the wealthy manipulating us I would hope that Brexit is the political reawakening of the British working classes. This genie does not go back into the bottle even if the political classes find a way to suffocate Brexit (and we can see they are trying desperately). Change is coming.

I also loathe the accusation that leave voters are uneducated as if the lack of education has produced an uneducated judgement in the referendum (i.e. 'stupid'). What is more likely is that the less educated are those in the less well-paying jobs, who have seen living standards reduce as a result of mass immigration. Those with greater education are likely to be more insulated from the immediate effects of mass immigration and are therefore less exposed. It is actually more 'stupid' of the remain voter not to see the unsustainability of mass immigration to society, and the economic and social burden it is placing upon their fellow 'uneducated' countrymen. Remain is a short-term and selfish vote.

'Russian Money. Unfair funding'. I love this one – because we were not influenced by the dirty money of Cameron and Osbourne's project fear leaflet (millions of taxpayer's money don't forget!), we are being influenced by Putin. Yes, because of all the positions I've outlined above are clearly driven by Russian interests. If it was the USSR then I could see the logic – 'international socialism, Tovarisch'!

It doesn't matter who financed the leave argument – British society does not work for many within Britain. We have voted for change. If this creates a small opportunity for Russia within its foreign policy with Europe then it is a price to be borne by all of those who refused to listen for the last two decades. We are still members of NATO. I don't recall the EU fighting any wars or keeping Russia at bay. Indeed, the bravado with which the EU courted Ukraine is one of the causes of the reawakening of an aggressive Russian foreign policy. Also, don't forget Cameron trying to rope in good ol' Nobel Prize winner Barack Obama to counsel the British public on the right way to vote. People will vote for all sorts of reasons, but Russia had no undue influence over our vote, any more than the money of big business and vested interests did over Remain voters.

Northern Ireland – In fairness this is a mess. This was not a major consideration of many voters as it was rarely discussed in the majority of conversations (at least not in Essex). It presents a significant problem and there is no easy way to navigate it. My own personal view is that the people of the island of Ireland deserve some assistance from the people of mainland Britain. If there was any way possible I would be seeking to flip the backstop on its head so that the UK has the backstop but the six counties remain in a customs union with the Republic of Ireland (and by extension the EU). Yes, it pushes the UK border into the sea but that is not logistically insurmountable. We could give dual passports to persons born and raised in NI. They have had the worst of living in the UK for a 100 years (various peoples' fault), so I see no harm in trying to give them the best of the 21st century – particularly if it can maintain friendly relations between the UK and the EU. If this is not workable then I would propose some sort of Hong Kong style Special Autonomous Region, where the SAR exists within the EU, complying with all EU Common Market practice but returning all taxes collected to the UK, less a small handling fee. It's not ideal but must be preferable to a hard border. It's not possible to police a hard border and may expose the UK to smuggling more than the Republic of Ireland (particularly people smuggling, though I'm sure many already have a plan to purchase cheaper food and goods from around the world to the UK which could be driven through Ireland for distribution in the EU). At least a border in the sea provides the rest of the UK with a more workable border. If we could agree a proposal with the EU then it could be put to a vote within Northern Ireland. They voted to remain after all. Is this the start of the break-up of the Union? Yes, quite possibly. Do I want Brexit to lead to a break-up of the Union? No, of course not, but I accept it is a risk. However, if the positive change we hope to see in the UK comes to pass hopefully Scotland, Wales and Northern Ireland will wish to remain. It would be hypocritical of me to want power closer to home, and not recognise that the working classes of Wales, Scotland and

Northern Ireland would want the same. A Federal UK would be preferable to the existing system where Scotland gets free education despite English taxpayers paying more per head, and Scotland benefitting from having both representatives in Holyrood and Westminster.

A cheeky alternative to Brexit perhaps – England votes to leave the UK?

Summary

So, whether you believe the logic is correct or not you can see that a logic exists. However, there is no argument that is impervious to criticism or can't be challenged. Brexit is not a single issue subject, and the experience of the individual voter will obviously determine their selection. Rather it should be seen holistically on both sides of the argument. One side the glass is half full – 'yes, there are problems but we can work them out together'. One side the glass is half empty – 'nothing will change for the better, and things will continue to get worse unless something drastic is done'. We have come to a fork in the road, and most people are emotionally entrenched on one side or the other. Logic applies, but so does emotion.

I can't see how Remain can demonstrate to ordinary persons why the benefits of EU membership outweigh the costs. I think it will certainly be difficult to prove the latter unless there is a major redistribution of wealth in the UK.

Brexit, Trump and the Yellow Jackets in France are warnings from the future. This is what happens when your government and wealthier classes are prepared to pursue a social and economic agenda that only benefits a narrow element of society.

Amid concerns regarding rising populism throughout the Western World, the working classes earnings as a % of costs have reduced significantly, and working people feel less optimism for the future than the past. The EU is not the sole cause of this, but the mishandling of the access of the A10 East European workers into the UK by Labour has exacerbated the challenge in the UK.

Immigration, whether positive or not to society, if not felt to be positive by the individual, will forever be entwined in that individual's mind with EU membership. Now, I accept there are means to manage it via ID cards and removal of universal benefits, but I fear the damage has been done in leave voters' minds. Freedom of movement has no logical benefit to the working classes of the UK as outlined previously. Only a tiny % will ever benefit from it. Therefore immigration needs to be resolved to win back leave voters who feel their quality of life has reduced as a result of it. Smearing people with accusations of racism offers no explanation of why those with an anti-immigration position are wrong. Even if we flip this argument on its head and say, 'do you know what – you are right – 17 million plus UK voters are racist, and solely voted leave because of their racist nature', where does that leave you? Will you shout 'racist!' at them forever until they learn the error of their ways, or will you seek to change their perceptions through concrete evidence of the benefit of immigration to the individual concerned? If you can't do that then you are left with trying to explain the benefits of migration on a macro-economic level, which isn't an easy argument when any growth in GDP is not being spread equally, combined with the dilution of resources by virtue of the increased headcount.

The view of the working classes fuelling 'populism' globally is very simple – fix our problems first. Not business' problems, not foreign citizens' problems, not the wealthier classes who are financially insulated. I struggle to understand the refusal of politicians to follow this. Have they been bought by business' desire to force down labour costs through mass immigration or do they truly believe mass immigration comes with no negative social impacts? The British working class is predominantly white but is also made up of BAME British – the need to fix their problems is as great in those communities as elsewhere. Constantly conflating the anti-immigration argument with accusations of racism is completely missing the point and can only be deliberate as there is no argument that can win over individuals experiencing a decline in living standards. Indeed, Brexit is not simply a reactionary, racist cry from the white working classes. There are towns throughout the UK where the demographics are different and also voted leave. Luton (56.5%), Hillingdon (56.4%), Slough (54.3%) and Bradford (54.2%) by way of example which have significant BAME populations. All races can be left behind by the elite.

Brexit has not created a schism in society. Anybody from a working class background knew the schism was already there – life is getting harder, and whilst each individual will have their own reasons for their vote, it ultimately comes down to a society fractured between haves and have nots. Those it works for, and those it doesn't. You cannot expect a society to agree upon a course of action when one element of society is on a positive trajectory and one is on a negative trajectory. It is the inevitable pinch point of globalisation – capital seeking greater returns forces the working classes of all countries into competition with one another. It is a fight to the bottom and will leave the poor in relatively wealthy countries more exposed as they obtain no economic benefit from migrating to those countries whose economies are providing a better return from their labour. Consider if the former workers from shipyards in the north east had left for Korea in the 60s. Aside from not being able to communicate and therefore not secure work, had they have been able to they would now be working class in Korea. Their money would be worth little in Korea let alone back in the UK. In contrast immigrants to the UK from poorer countries can return their working class wages to the mother country, and upskill their English – the global Lingua Franca.

Irrespective of Brexit, if we want a more unified society we need more unified wealth. This doesn't require a move away from capitalism, but it requires the political classes to manage the unequal outcomes of capitalism and the negative societal effects it produces. There are obvious ways to do this. A public recognition from politicians that twenty-six people own as much wealth as 50% of the planet is grotesque would be a start **(Oxfam).**

It should also be publicly recognised that these people did not earn that wealth. They were the lucky beneficiaries of a systemic flaw. It is the structural flaws of capitalism that need to be more clearly recognised and fixed. There are positives to capitalism. Trade has undoubtedly created wealth for mankind. It reflects the development of a system that reflects human nature – the need to trade, to barter, specialisation of labour. Frankly, capitalism gives us all an excuse to get out of bed in the morning. We can make more, build more, sell more.

Taking aside the obviously devastating effect that capitalism has had on the environment, it is a system that works because it is easy to understand. It has also led to tremendous advancements in basic human health and wealth most obviously demonstrated through increased life expectancy and increased consumption.

The obvious flaw in capitalism, like any system, is that it has been gamed. Capitalism is no different to a game of monopoly. As long as we allow the existence of private assets, and for most societies in history this is a cultural norm, we provide benefits to one over another. Who made the land upon which we operate today? I can find out who owns the land, but they can have no logical argument for their ownership beyond that they bought it from somebody else in the past. It seems like a fair and reasonable argument. But trace it back and you will realise that somebody previously stole that land from God or nature. Those owning that land will have sold it to pursue other economic opportunities, depriving all others beyond the new owner of its natural use. Start a game of monopoly with 7 billion players and follow it through to the logical conclusion. The structure of the game means that over time you will see that only a handful of players will own the board. Everybody else, whilst free to make their own decisions, will be financing those that own the board. If you think that my analogy is weak or misunderstands capitalism then I redirect you to another statement from **Oxfam – the world's richest 1% bagged 82% percent of wealth created last year (2017).**

Another myth that should be expunged regarding capitalism is that people are rewarded for their efforts or hard work.

However, we are all limited by twenty-four hours a day. It's a universal, scientific law. Nobody can work beyond that yet we see CEOs paid thousands of times more than those in junior positions. Are they really working harder?

Alternatively we can take the view that whilst those being most heavily rewarded are not working harder, they are working smarter. However, the performance of CEOs is invariably mixed. If a new appointee was to implement nothing would their impact be greater or lesser than if the share price of the company just ebbed and flowed on the tide of the global economy? Yes, leadership is required, but can no leadership be better than bad leadership? The poor performance of numerous CEOs suggests that they are by no means working smarter than those below them.

If you were to stand back and look at the structure of most companies you can see an obvious pyramid, with many low paid employees at the bottom, with income rising to very few at the top. This is the self-fulfilling prophecy that makes us all accept the system. Like buying a lottery ticket because we know somebody has to win. Somebody has to be in the boss' chair at some point in the future. However, the odds are massively stacked against you irrespective of effort or intelligence.

Another argument is that those who are wealthy are wealth creators. They have taken risks. I've never understood this argument. If capitalism had not been gamed this may be true. However, one of the key vehicles of all business' development is the limited nature of their exposure. The clue is in the name of virtually all business' – 'Limited'. Whenever anybody sets out on a fantastic new capitalist adventure they know exactly what they are going to lose. They are not taking a risk with their own money, but with the banks who they have sold a vision to. The profit is privatised whilst the risk is socialised. You might question how the risk is socialised, and again, in a true form of capitalism it wouldn't be, but in our gamed version of capitalism you can see how this plays out. The 2008 financial crash meant that governments had to act as the lender of last resort to banks and other major financial investors who supported reckless overlending to clearly indebted individuals who couldn't pay it back.

The banks will argue they didn't have visibility on who they were lending to because of the opaque nature of packaged debts they were taking on – but this then raises the point of why are they so handsomely rewarded? If all you are doing is backing the market, what added value are you providing as an industry? Where is the hard work, the smart work or the talent in not knowing what they were buying? Or, even worse, they knew what they were buying was junk but didn't care because they were too big to fail. Again, no intelligence or talent but simply being able to operate in an exalted position of protection where the law of supply and demand that is used to justify cost cuts to ordinary people somehow never seems to apply to those at the top.

Another key consideration when it comes to wealth is luck and timing. Take Facebook. Mark Zuckerberg is clearly a clever guy, but he didn't invent the internet, or computer code or even social media. He happened to be at university at the same time as others who all built upon developments before them. Yes, they are clever people, and yes, they were no doubt working hard, but without eighty years of prior development behind him throughout the sphere of computer technology would he have developed Facebook out of thin air? Would anybody? Does he deserve to be richer than God? I am sure if you follow the development of technology there will be countless developers who made astronomical leaps who received no more than their annual wage. Mark Zuckerberg could have been anybody – he just happened to be the right person, in the right place at the right time. Don't forget Friends Reunited and Myspace already existed and over time would have evolved into almost the same thing as Facebook. This is a single example, but whenever people justify individual wealth they fail to consider how timing or luck play a part.

I have been told that luck is simply preparation meeting opportunity. That may well be true but what it sure as hell demonstrates is that most of us will never be lucky enough to hit that sweet spot no matter how hard we work. It should also be considered how 'luck' reflects the changing nature of industries. If you happen to be in an industry in a period of unprecedented growth that is not yet understood by financial markets who are desperate to avoid missing out, does that make your rewards justified? Or does it simply represent rather than talent or success, you literally were in the right place at the right time – Y2K consultants for example? Early investors in Bitcoin?

Capitalism works because we all buy into the idea that effort generates reward, but clearly it doesn't. On average, it will no doubt play a part, but the exceptional wealth rewarded to fortunate individuals can no longer be acceptable.

You may say that wealth doesn't bring happiness and I can see that every time I pick up a newspaper and see another celebrity relationship in the bin. However, wealth does buy undue influence and it is this which ultimately has gamed democracy. If our political systems dictate our economic system, then it would be in the interest of the wealthy to seek to secure and develop their positions via the political system. Surely democracy is not in the pockets of wealthy interests? How can it be when each person has one vote and companies have none? How could the working class, the base of the triangle, the biggest number on the ballot box, be voting against their own interests? **Because the system has been gamed.**

You only get access to the political system once every five years. I don't mean local government but real power. Once every five years. And yet, companies have access via lobbyists on a daily basis. You can send a letter to your MP whilst lobbyists are pressuring them on a daily basis with opaque agreements that smack of corruption. By the time you get your vote in five years' time society has taken another step further away from you and you solely get to choose from the least of the worst options.

Lobbying cannot be allowed. Corruption cannot be allowed. If the system is to work for everybody then we have to have equal access – that access is once every five years for all. If lobbyists want to make their arguments they should do them in the public eye to try to win the support of the people to their argument. If it is logical it will win support. If not, then it will fail.

'You'd be richer if you worked harder' is a common response. The above demonstrates clearly that you wouldn't. There are only twenty-four hours in a day. 'You should have tried harder at school'. I love this one. It suggests that if we all got firsts from Oxbridge we'd all be rich. UK society does not have tens of millions of professional level jobs out there for Oxbridge graduates. We would simply have a society of millions of professionally educated persons for the handful of professional level jobs that exist.

Even when the government claims to be doing something positive, its true cause appears to be private profit and societal debt. Look at Labour's 'education, education, education'. More people than ever going to university to what end? More people in debt and no more professional jobs. And to top it all off, we're going to invite millions of East Europeans at all levels from professors to labourers to block your access to the labour market. Enjoy your education kid!

Think about how this is financed – students in debt via ever increasing loans. (Thanks Lib Dems! They might want democracy but they don't want equality – let's keep education to those who can afford it.) This is either a private debt on the masses, or if it is never paid back it is a societal debt against the taxpayer. Who is benefitting – we now have places like Grays Thurrock University F.F.S., appearing to generate wonky degrees for immigrants to scam visas. Look at the chancellor of Bath University earning 468k!

Think about house prices – banks are allowed to loosen lending criteria. Who does this benefit? The wealthy can now extend their purchasing power pushing up prices. They were already sitting at the top but now they'll stretch even further – everybody else now entering the market has to dig even deeper. Come back to our monopoly board and you can see how the generational wealth problem has occurred. Those sitting on properties gained from purchasers having ACCESS to more money. They didn't have more money, they hadn't earnt more money. They were simply able to access more. However, this money was just debt going into the pockets of big business. Every day property prices rise as wages fail to keep up. This is because the system is gamed. Banks lobbied politicians and bought them via legal but morally corrupt practices. Why are so many knights of the realm former business people? Why do so many former ministers end up in executive positions with gold plated pensions? If the banking industry were to have pitched this to the public it would never have been accepted.

Even if private lobbying were made illegal, who do you think controls the lobbying of you, the voter? On a daily basis you are fed a diatribe of views and opinions designed to influence you. This ranges from products they want you to buy to your thoughts on societal norms. No matter how clever you are, you will be influenced, or you will be affected by those influenced around you. If you don't agree then consider why the global spend on advertising in 2019 is 562 billion USD **(statista.com)**.

Clearly advertisers are clever people but they can't have pulled the wool over so many other clever people's eyes for so long if it didn't matter.

You yourself are being gamed and it is impossible to resist. It wouldn't be so bad if we were educated enough to at least apply some critical reasoning or thinking to challenge this, but the level and quality of education seems to be deteriorating. It is almost by design.

It is going to get worse as digital consumption means you will not benefit from other's critical thinking. At least in the past you could benefit from the fact that published statements in newspapers and media would be scrutinised by all and challenged. Not that it helped fight tides of money but it at least kept the debate within the confines of the truth. The internet takes unchallenged ideas into all areas of our lives, and I can understand the fear of those who see it driving populism. I see populism as the pushback against the undue influence of wealth and bought systems, rather than the enforcement of it, but I can fully accept the concern.

Even before we had unchallenged social media, we had the mainstream media. For decades the mass media has been feeding us all a message in favour of liberalised economics and low taxes as being the norm. Look what this has resulted in – housing crisis for young people, failing services for all of us, increasing crime and ultimately a decreasing quality of life for nearly everybody. During that time media empires have moved from being national to international, mirroring or driving globalisation at the expense of the working classes in

83

the developed world. Yet these persons have no interest in the society in which you live. Of course they are interested in sales, but they are just as motivated by power. Look at the rush of senior politicians to curry favour with scumbag media moguls over the last couple of decades. Like him or loathe him, Jeremy Corbyn is not in the pockets of these people and is attacked on a daily basis because of it. The owners of this media are invariably foreign based or tax exiles driving the agenda of our country whilst paying very little tax in it. This has to stop. Any entity seeking to influence the debate in this country has to be majority owned in this country. They have to be paying tax in this country. We cannot have persons with so little to lose having so much influence. It is the same as lobbying. No more involvement between politicians and the press. If you as a politician wish to speak to Murdoch you do it publicly and on the record. Let it be critically assessed by all, particularly the rival press. Anything else has to be illegal otherwise you are accepting that democracy is not one person, one vote every five years, but a phone call to the PM for some and not for others. Democracy does not work unless access to power is equal for all.

This brings us to the crux of the issue of Brexit – how did we get here? How did we get to a position where the country is so irrevocably split on a fundamental issue? It represents the failure of our political system to represent the interest of anybody other than the politicians and those financing the politicians.

Would mass immigration have occurred had there been a referendum? No. Would financial deregulation have occurred had there been a referendum? No. Would the UK be so integrated with the EU that I cannot now extricate itself without causing existential harm had there been a referendum? No. Would council house sell off and privatisation of national assets been allowed had there been a referendum? No. The failure of the British political system is that it grants the government more power than the support they have generated in society. This all comes down to the electoral system.

Think about it. As I stated above we understand our version of parliamentary democracy as being one person one vote. That is true but the principle is then twisted to result in the majority of votes being wasted in most constituencies. Look at the figures below for Thurrock – the winning MP represents less than 34% of the electorate. That means that 2/3 of the electorate have no representation. How can society progress when the views of the clear majority of people are not being considered at parliament?

2015 General Election: Thurrock

	Votes	%	±
Conservative	16,692	33.7	Decrease 3.1%
Labour	16,156	32.6	Decrease 4%
UKIP	15,718	31.7	Increase 24.3%
Liberal Democrat	644	1.3	Decrease 9.4%

This means the majority of UK voters have no representation. How can that ever be a logical system and who is it intended to benefit?

It is worth considering the origins of our parliamentary system. As landowners, and subsequently industrialists, fought to seize power from monarchs, they developed a system whereby executive power was divided between the monarch and the elite of society. This elite did not have the time to commit to negotiating power plays in Westminster, so would employ 'representatives' on their behalf. Modern MPs are simply the latest manifestation of that. Representatives of their financiers. Agents of the establishment, not the people.

Consider the fairness of a system that in 2015 returned the following:

Table: 2015 General Election results summary

	Seats	Votes	%
Conservative	331	11,334,920	36.9
Labour	232	9,347,326	30.4
Scottish National	56	1,454,436	4.7
Liberal Democrat	8	2,415,888	7.9
Democratic Unionist	8	184,260	0.6
Sinn Féin	4	176,232	0.6
Plaid Cymru	3	181,694	0.6
SDLP	3	99,809	0.3
Ulster Unionist	2	114,935	0.4
UKIP	1	3,881,129	12.6
Green	1	1,157,613	3.8
Others	1	164,826	0.5

And imagine how many more people do not vote because they live in safe seats? No wonder the electorate is so disengaged with politics when they are so disenfranchised. No wonder they want to kick those in power in a fair, one person one vote that counts election, such as the Brexit referendum. You may not have liked the result of the referendum but you have to accept it was fair. Compare this to the ordinary general elections and consider whether this represents fairness. Look at the above.

The Tories got a seat for every 34,000 votes. UKIP got one seat for 4 million votes!

SNP got a seat for every 26,000 votes. Their supporters are disproportionately driving the political agenda of the UK. The only fair election we have ever had in this country – one person, one vote in the Brexit referendum and look at the result. The establishment lose. Why does the establishment exist and why does it always win? Just like the house always wins in a casino – because the odds have been rigged in their favour.

The way to change the injustice in this country that has given rise to Brexit starts with fixing the electoral system. Imagine if Nigel Farage or similar had been able to exert some influence twenty years ago. The UK would have been unlikely to sign up to Maastricht and many of the current problems would not exist. The UK could have been on the periphery of the EU as a valued trading and security partner. Now, even when a vote to leave has taken place, we cannot extricate ourselves because the tentacles are so tight.

For a fairer society we need the electorate's vote to matter and be proportionally represented. We need only the electorate to have access to politicians – no more lobbyists.

If companies and lobbyists have valid arguments as to why to favour their industry or proposed legislation then argue it to the people. The extremes of capitalism would soon stop if the political system was not bought. It would enforce the need for compromise which would smooth out the extremes of the last fifty years. From Thatcherism onwards the UK has suffered from political and economic convulsions that would not have occurred in such an extreme manner had the people been more represented in power. Look at the situation we now find ourselves in – working people being made homeless. Working people unable to afford rent and being able to buy property becoming a dream. Households requiring all adults to work just to stand still. All the time the rich are getting proportionally richer, and it is not through their efforts or hard work but the structural advantages that exist within capitalism and are supported and maintained by the ruling parties.

Brexit, and other forms of populism throughout the West, must be taken as a warning. The rise of artificial intelligence (AI) threatens an even greater challenge to the working classes than austerity. Jobs will be lost. I keep being told that it's not a problem as technology will create jobs that don't even exist today so people should embrace the upcoming job losses as they will move into better roles. Sure. Remember when you could get a local job in your high street working in retail? You got to have a job, with a pension, in your local community. Now you get to work in a warehouse loading trolleys or driving a van for zero hours contracts with absolutely no security. Thank you technology! Whilst those owning the technology are based in a foreign country and paying zero tax in the UK, whilst the country supports their economic gains. Again – the privatisation of profit and the socialisation of cost. This is unsustainable.

The more people feel disconnected with the future the less they have to lose with regards crime and violence. We already have a situation where violent criminals are not being investigated or caught, and even when they are, they are not being imprisoned because it's too costly. When does the tipping point come? Why should anybody follow the rules? How far is the ordinary taxpayer going to be pushed before they look for alternatives at the extreme end? We are experiencing reduced access to healthcare, education and reduced access to justice. If this trajectory continues then we do risk some of the hyperbole spoken about Brexit actually coming to pass. If people are pushed into extreme positions they will start to consider extreme responses.

Brexit is our opportunity to understand the frustrations of what too many in our society are experiencing and consider how to rectify them before the opportunity is taken away from us.

How to repair UK society

Immigration

Immigration has to be controlled. Irrespective of whether the UK remains in the EU or not, mass immigration has to cease and be replaced with a skills based test. No more immigrants below professional level. We do not need dishwashers. If our own population won't do the job then there is something wrong with that industry's economic model. We should not be supporting an unsustainable business through unfair competition within the workforce. If the jobs are of strategic national importance – i.e. farming – then government subsidies will need to be applied to help such industries. However, there can be no excuse for the UK providing NHS healthcare and other public welfare support to non-UK persons who are not net contributors. We're already seeing the Tories trying to support big business by stating that Theresa May's post-Brexit GBP 30k minimum wage requirement is too high. Of course it is – it is meant to be a barrier for entry for a good reason. We need quality over quantity. We want our immigrants to be professors, engineers, entrepreneurs. We want them to be operating within niches of society that our education system is simply too slow to respond to. We want them to upskill our workforce and we want them to add value to society.

Refugees need help. We should help them. But does accepting refugees from the next continent really make sense or is it simply economic migration wearing a plaster cast? Surely rather than financing a very difficult mass immigration to Europe, with the inevitable cultural and economic difficulties of people being poorly educated and competing with struggling domestic populations, we should finance them in neighbouring countries. Rather than have Syrians in the UK why can't we finance them in towns in Jordan or Turkey? Migrants could live in houses and towns where the cost of housing, healthcare and education is significantly lower than in the UK. Those who are economically viable will contribute to the new country and those who aren't can be supported by Western Governments. Then, when the conflicts in the region subside, people can return home with new, and viable, commercial relationships in the neighbouring country raising the economic wealth of the region.

If we are going to survive we need to start dealing with issues at a macro level and not a micro level. We build a process, invest in that process, and make clear there will be no exceptions permitted. The problem with illegal migration is that it cheats the genuine migrants – those who are waiting in line in poor countries – trying to study and to obtain visas. It also creates animosity amongst the working classes in wealthier countries which in turns fuels anti-immigration policies making it harder for the genuine immigrants in poorer countries to get in.

There is no test of quality for illegal immigrants, no establishing credentials or qualifications. They are also in competition with the domestic working class of the country they have entered. I have read many stories of 'my father is my hero – he worked two jobs as an illegal immigrant'. On a personal, micro level that is magnificent and should be applauded. A man who will do anything for his family. On a macro level it is a disaster. Two domestic workers were deprived of job opportunities. The immigrant is paid in cash with no tax contributions because, the clue is in the name, they are illegal and cannot pay tax. The two domestic workers deprived of jobs may now be requiring welfare support. To then consider granting amnesty to illegal immigrants simply rubs the nose in all other parties trying to progress by following the rules. I understand it may cost more to send illegal migrants back, but the cost of not doing so is to undermine the rule of law and the concept of fairness. Worse, it sets the precedent to the next wave of 5 billion economic migrants that they should simply get to the West and to hell with the rules.

Piecemeal responses to immigration are not helping. Let's ease the challenges on a macro level via global co-operation using declining populations. For example, if wealthy people in India need old age support they will pay more for staff if India shifts to an ageing population. It is a genuine example of trickle-down economics because those at the bottom of society hold the supply. Trickle-down economics as championed by Reagan and Thatcher can never work when those at the top can keep securing services from the lowest possible bidder when there is unlimited supply (i.e. mass immigration, or globalisation). However, if you limit supply at the bottom you can use it to effectively transfer wealth. It also helps to avoid issues of inheritance unfairness as the working classes will be able to secure a larger share of total wealth.

Less focus on Identity Politics

We need to stop splintering society and the working class by focusing on identity politics. This is not a cry against political correctness which is purely seeking to encourage mindfulness, rather a call for the working classes to recognise the real obstacle to their progression – the system and how it is maintained. However, identity politics acts as a useful distraction for the establishment as the working classes are split amongst competing interest groups – white vs. non-white, male vs. female, old vs. young. The white working class will always rail against this and appear reactionary because they perceive it as an unfair advantage. The BAME population will understandably confuse that 100% of British political and economic power is held by white people as being 100% of white people having an institutional advantage over non-white persons.

For me one of the failings of Britain's multiracial society is that many BAME citizens perceive their disadvantaged position as being a result of racism. What they are missing is the fact that there are tens of millions of white Britains in the same position. If your parents came to the UK to clean dishes in a restaurant you are unlikely to become a high court judge. It's not due to your colour or religion – it is the law of averages applied against your start in life. Too much of the upper echelons of UK life is dominated by those who are privately educated **(Elitist Britain 2019 – The Sutton Trust)**. They already come from wealth and yet get a better education than everybody else. Society is gamed in their favour. But because of a recent focus on race as somehow representing diversity, people are mistaking white with wealthy. Why are all judges white? Racial discrimination! Maybe, but surely the issue should be why are all judges privately educated when they only represent 1% of the population?

I saw Sir Lenny Henry make a point recently about why there were not enough BAME producers in the arts. Well, Lenny, could it be because such positions are invariably held by the wealthy and privately educated and yes, they may be mostly white, but they are also wealthy. If Daddy is a Nigerian prince and owns an insurance company in Nigeria, I would suggest it is damn well racism if you can't get a job in insurance in the City of London. If you are a black kid from East Ham whose Nigerian father worked on the factory floor in Ford's in Dagenham, then not securing a job in insurance in The City is more likely to reflect your individual educational and social background. You are in the same boat as all the other kids in East London raised in working class backgrounds – irrespective of race, your future success, *on average*, is guided by your socio-economic position at birth.

I saw another statistic about the % of management of the NHS that were BAME being far less than the overall % of BAME staff within the NHS. Well, of course. The majority of BAME persons are working class. You are experiencing the difficulties of being British working class – you are not experiencing racism. By allowing mass immigration of low skilled workers we are creating a potential division in society along lines of race and culture when the reality is they are hamstrung by their socio-economic start in life. This is then compounded because they perceive their failure to be due to racial and cultural issues rather than structural issues concerning wealth and opportunity. We risk fighting each other when the answer is staring us in the face – your opportunities are limited by your socio-economic background. Indeed, most reports show that the white working class have the lowest educational attainment of all social groups **(Sutton Trust).**

When striving for diversity we have to start with economic opportunity – race should not be a factor, because determining somebody's worth by their race is surely racism? Determining somebody's worth by their gender is surely sexism? You are splitting people on a single aspect of their person to the benefit or cost of all others.

I guess the explanation is that it's low hanging fruit. Organisations wish to be seen as diverse so seek BAME persons to demonstrate how diverse they are. But if every woman, BAME person and homosexual in the board room is privately educated are you really getting diversity? Or are you just getting different paintjobs on luxury cars?

As a white, working class, straight male, am I surely not a more diverse figure in the boardroom than the homosexual son of an African prince who was educated at Eton? I'll let you consider your own view on that – it's a personal opinion, with no right and wrong, but we need to be careful of where thinking of diversity in terms of only one small part of a person's being leads to. Surely we are all individuals with our own strengths and weaknesses? If we are not, then surely stupid generalisations on the basis of gender, race and religion start to become more justified. 'Black people are this', 'gay people are that', 'women are this', 'Muslims are that'. People are either individuals and need to be assessed as such, or they are defined by a single genetic characteristic. You can't have it both ways. The way to achieve true diversity is to push for diversity on a class, or socio-economic basis, as this will naturally engender a true diversity. My concern is that the push for diversity simply reflects a middle management media view on diversity – a tick box exercise that leaves all working class constituents frustrated as the big picture questions are never raised, and the status quo is never challenged.

If representation is demanded solely on the basis of a single characteristic could a situation arise where the % of BAME persons in roles that are over-representative of their position in society are challenged – acting, sport etc. Should we accept quotas and forced diversity on this basis? Should we suggest a diversion in funding when diversity targets are met? Race alone does not represent diversity. Sexuality alone does not represent diversity. Religion alone does not represent diversity.

Socio economics encompasses diversity and it is that divide that needs to be bridged to ensure equality of opportunity for all – not some middle-class kid who doesn't need a break because they happen to tick a diversity box. It is these frustrations that have left the white working classes feeling ostracised. Labour seems to have given up on fighting for the working class as a whole and seems to be focused on identity politics, which only benefit a certain % of the working class. As I stated above it seems like they are seeking to grab low hanging fruit. A few easy wins in terms of 'diversity representation' by employing a female, BAME or LGBT professional from a privately educated background rather than a white male professional from a privately educated background to show progress.

So now the working classes are even more blocked – their opportunity to progress is being stalled because of racial or sexual inverse discrimination. Diversity is simply a justification to keep the working classes out whilst appearing to be fair. True representation, like my point about democracy, should see the % of roles reflect the population. To take Sir Lenny Henry's point, if 80% of the population are white working class, then 80% of high court judges should be white working class. That is what we need to be aiming for. However, do you want your aeroplane engineer to have got the position on the basis of their knowledge or their diversity? If only 20% of working class kids make it to university, only a certain % of aircraft engineers are going to be working class. It is an ambition but it will take generations to correct and requires a levelling of the playing field. Social mobility is what we want – a true meritocracy. How do you achieve it?

A very simple question to you dear reader – are rich kids cleverer? Yes or No? You either accept there is a genetic difference which is unlikely but could be true – parents are likely to have been attracted to one another on the basis of shared intellect or social status. However, that then needs to be adjusted for prior generation's achievements. I don't know the answer to the question I raised but I strongly believe the answer is that a parent's wealth doesn't dictate the intelligence of an offspring but it sure as hell influences their life opportunities.

We need to find a way to make society like golf. If you had a privileged upbringing you get a handicap. But this does then bring me back to my point about how skilled do you want your aeronautical engineer to be when you board a plane. How skilled do you want the pilot to be?

As an analogy - Formula One suffers when the technological leap made by one car distorts the competition. You are unsure whether it is Jenson Button's driving that won him the world title or Ross Brawn's motor engineering. The same would be true in society. What we need is for everybody to drive the same car. But, even if we all drove the same car, some kids will have been taking driving lessons since birth whilst others will have never been in a car. The system will be gamed so that some start the race on pole position.

It's difficult to make everybody equal. If we accept that everybody is different then why would you judge diversity on the basis of such limited characteristics as race, gender or sexuality? The white people at the top of society invariably reflect that until recently Britain was an almost fully white country. There are generations of wealth amassed amongst those people that is used to retain their wealth and insulate their positions in society. Most BAME immigrants (though by no means all) will not have entered the UK at the equivalent level of the British establishment. Therefore, why would they expect to have the same outcome when the odds are so clearly stacked against them?

When we try to level the playing field let's do it for everybody – not particular characteristics which just create increased division. Diversity is not a positive term as it naturally excludes many who are already excluded. Let's strive for a society of inclusivity where we open the doors to everybody who is currently locked out, for all reasons.

Equal Representation

How do you level the playing field? You start with a voting system which is truly representative. No votes can be wasted anymore. Brexit has shown us that a society divided economically cannot move forward as one. We cannot negotiate externally when we have no common position internally.

Secondly, you ensure that wealth no longer purchases exception – no lobbying and no foreign ownership of mass media. If you want to comment on the UK's problems you have to reside in the UK and understand the problems. To enforce this there should be no private donations to political parties beyond membership fees. If you can't survive without your members then clearly you are not representative of UK society. There can be no undue influence being brought to bear on our politicians. If our politicians are bought then what are they good for? Why not use technology for every vote – a referendum on every decision via the internet? Direct democracy in its truest sense. It's something to aim for, but to start with we need to clean the existing system up.

Thirdly – no exceptions on tax. Why do the working classes have to be paid PAYE yet the professional classes are able to be paid to then divert their income to offshore havens? No more ability to offset taxes. This only benefits those who have the funds to finance exceptions.

Fourthly – work has to pay more than wealth. How can capital gains tax be lower than income tax? How can the talented in the working class ever expect to become wealthy when existing wealth is taxed at a lower rate than earnings via employment? How can somebody renting a flat out earn more than somebody working twelve hours a day? If this means more onerous taxes on wealth then it is appropriate to recognise the need to level the playing field. One of the problems with the EU is that it is a tax professional's dream. Wealth and earnings can be transferred to the lowest possible tax regime, favouring those countries whose populations and societies have far lower cost structures. The same applies in our societies. How can individuals making money from property in London be able to pay tax on that income in the Cayman Islands? One of the factors that enables a property in London to have such earning potential is that the UK has a stable society financed through taxation. The health system, the education system, the emergency services, the councils, all ensure a standard of life that supports the wealth making capability of London and other UK towns and cities. That is what makes the flat an attractive proposition for a rental investment. It is not acceptable for a person or company to benefit from the costs of maintaining a healthy society without them making a contribution to it.

If the US had a revolution on the basis of no tax without representation, we need the same – no societal benefits to you or your organisation without taxation being paid. You cannot have a business operating in the UK, that reaps the benefits of being in the UK, yet pay no tax in the UK.

This has to be apply to the personal and the professional. Any earnings in the UK, whether via the internet or not, have to be taxed here to reflect the contribution that the UK pays to the provision of the earnings. Think of how somebody like Amazon utilises the UK road system to make its deliveries. Do they contribute their fair share in tax in the UK or do they redirect their profits to a more favourable tax jurisdiction?

The push for globalisation only seems to benefit those at the top. Why is that? Because it is being pushed for by lobbyists who have a plan and a priced and funded strategy. Where does this leave you, dear citizen, as the jobs are exported to lower margin countries? It leaves you at best in a more precarious position than previously, and at worse on the scrap heap. We can have faith that technology will produce new jobs, but if all of the money generated by that technology goes to offshore tax havens society will not be able to financially support those who have suffered redundancy. Alternatively the tax rate will have to become more burdensome on those that do earn, but to what end if they reach a tipping point and decide it's no longer economical to continue to work?

To clarify, I am talking about ordinary working people here, not those who might have the ability to offshore wealth. It's funny how the UK still tries to distinguish things on class backgrounds to determine how cultured or educated somebody is. The only class that matters is economic. If you have to work for your income you are working class, irrespective of your knowledge of quinoa or recognising difference between ironic facial hair and high street adopters. The middle class are simply working class persons with options. They may feel that their education, knowledge and savings or assets protects them from the wrath of big business but it won't for long. All of the challenges being felt by the working classes which have led to a Brexit vote of frustration will start to come for you too. I hope that middle-class professional Remainers trumpeting open borders and free access to the NHS for foreign nationals ('it would be racist to charge' – BMA 26th June 2019) remember this when it is their jobs lost or industries destroyed.

The irony is that capitalism's biggest strength will be its destruction. The failure to price societal costs into a business decision will end up with a society unable to operate. Yes, a balance sheet will plan for tax and will seek to legally minimise its exposure, but like the earlier monopoly analogy, play the game for ever and you end up with a winning company in a society that can no longer function. No police, no healthcare, no education. You can mitigate against these for a while by paying your staff more to be able to access private versions – your staff can live in gated communities, with private healthcare and education, but sooner or later you create a society where you can't trust your cook or driver or nurse not to rob you, or worse your family.

The decision to offshore jobs and profit has been supported by our governments for decades and for what end? A broken society that is just getting worse. This is multiplied to the nth degree when you consider the failure of capitalism to consider the cost of environmental destruction on its balance sheets.

Environmental

Above I touched on some strategic methods to build a fairer society. Next I want to talk about how we could link environmental policies with redistribution of wealth.

I have faith that technology will save the planet – necessity is the mother of invention after all, but human nature being what it is means that it will be left until the very last moment. By then the planet that we know and love may be essentially inhospitable for humankind to progress. The population may be so small and disparate that a plague could easily see us extinct.

However, to avoid that scenario lets pre-empt it. Let's consider how an equalling of wealth could lead to a fairer society and world. There will obviously be better persons than I to offer sustainable solutions, but I just want to get the ball rolling on some ideas.

Firstly – a planned population reduction. As noted above the capitalist concept of growth is essentially a Ponzi scheme. It does not guarantee an increased quality or productivity. In fact, the finite resources of the planet means that sooner or later growth will come to a cataclysmic halt anyway. If we could aim for a global population reduction would that not free up more housing in developed countries and reduced competition for jobs? Western countries would be as well setting up free healthcare in poorer nations to ensure better access to family planning and to ensure infant mortality rates match those in the West to help reduce the need for multiple children. So straight away you can see that on a global scale everybody can benefit. If we have the will and are prepared to share. In time you could aim for a population reduction so that issues such as immigration and nationality reduce. Free global movement of all persons could be achievable if we all had a similar cost of living. Why not aim for 2100 – no more nations beyond regions and accents? Two birds etc.

But, conversely, being overly generous and inviting the world in to Western countries does not help anybody as poorer countries would rely upon emigration as a means of generating wealth. This has to stop to enable poorer countries to prosper themselves and to relieve the pressure on working classes in richer nations. Isn't it funny how celebrities are always advocating open borders and one world? Is it because they are independently wealthy of society and therefore can move on if it goes pear shaped? I'd love to meet a celebrity that didn't think this because at least it would show some critical thinking. How could you not love everybody in the world when you are insulated from its pressures? You are not in competition with anybody once you are financially insulated. If somebody or somewhere is giving you grief, you just move on.

Perhaps we could have a country buddy system? Like town twinning but for countries. The richest country supports the poorest country with the aim of getting them to a certain level – free trade, free movement of people (though capped at reciprocal levels!), language and culture exchange.

Working practices. Another way to create a more egalitarian society through environmentalism is to consider working practices. A four-day week has regularly been discussed as a way of transferring wealth to the general population and this immediately brings a 20% gain to all workers in terms of rate per hour. However, how can we use this to benefit the environment? Well an immediate consideration would be to make the day off formal – a day for the environment. So, as we currently have 'The Weekend', we could develop 'Midweek' – every Wednesday people are off work but the payoff is no cars, limited electricity, no shops. It's like Sundays used to be. Public transport would be available but the day would need to be seen as a means of reducing environmental damage whilst preparing us all for a reduced energy future. People could focus on charity and local welfare schemes. 'Midweek' could be a day for mass participation in sports or politics. An opportunity for us to all refresh whilst reducing emissions. Of course there will be exceptions – emergency service workers for example, but then none of these persons work seven days a week so the opportunity would be to increase more part-time working. Three and a half days each a week. Imagine if every person over fifty-five has to reduce their working hours to 50% – it would guarantee that younger generations get to move up the earnings ladder, redistributing wealth. Perhaps for the first generation the state could keep pension contributions topped up to reflect that it will have impacted peoples financial planning, but it would stop the current situation where wealth seems too focused towards the older generations (recognising of course that the average person in each generation is not wealthy).

Another key economic and environmental target has to be to secure more local jobs. It breaks my heart when I see office blocks being converted to flats because it simply means more people for less jobs.

Unless a job requires a physical presence (i.e. a surgeon!) then the law needs to be changed to demand remote working. It will reduce fossil fuel consumption and it will assist workers to secure a better work life balance – producing greater opportunities for socially beneficial activities such as exercise (less NHS spend) and charity.

Similarly for start and finish times – work needs to be staggered by law. The individual gets to choose their start and finish times. Maybe a conventional office based nine to five becomes start between seven to eleven, to finish at three to seven. The purpose of this would be to reduce stress on roads and pollution caused by traffic blockages, but also to avoid the perverse situation of overcrowded public transport in one direction versus empty carriages in the other direction.

Having more flexible working and remote working would alleviate the housing crisis as people could live further afield from major towns and cities whilst having a more enjoyable transport situation when they do need to visit the office. It might also have the benefit of revitalising high streets. Even if just for coffee and lunch venues there would be so many more active consumers on any given day.

Of course businesses will be up in arms but this is an extinction threat level we need to respond to. Practical measures which can improve people's quality of life whilst saving the planet must be prioritised.

Even air travel could be used to redistribute wealth if the ambition is there. Who genuinely needs to fly when Skype exists? Yes, business is better face to face but there is no absolute requirement nowadays. Holidays – OK, but we should be looking at how we can all reduce our carbon footprint. Perhaps a way of doing it is to ration people to one ticket each. Those who can do without can sell to richer bidders, thus redistributing wealth. Each year the number of tickets available would reduce by 10%, allowing for a slow decline in the affected industries. Can you imagine the speed at which the airline operators will develop cleaner technologies if such a situation was enacted? And this means no private jets – no exceptions for wealth. If you have the money you can be grateful for the extra flights you can purchase via the ticket lottery winners, and learn to hold your nose. No more Emma Thompsons in first class please. No more Prince Harry twenty private flights a year whilst lecturing the rest of us. No more Elton John – 'Well I've paid to offset it', as though that makes it right. We need egalitarian environmentalism, something we can all believe in and know we are all participating in. My earlier point about pride in the Second World War – everybody fought together. This needs the same efforts. It will only happen though, if we know there are no exceptions bought by wealth or power. As soon as the exceptions are seen to exist then we're not in it together and anger and frustration grow. Remember David Cameron's statement re. George Osborne's austerity policy – 'we're all in it together'? It is bare-faced, arrogant lies like this from pampered, privileged elites that resulted in Brexit. Think how we will react when the world starts burning and flooding and you are looking for an exception for your wealth.

Relying on the efforts of individuals won't work without legislation, as Dame Emma will always believe that she is more worthy than the little people. Luxury has to end and a new era of egalitarianism has to occur to justify the reduction in lifestyle required to mitigate environmental disaster. This can't be like 2008 when Cameron famously lied that 'we are all in this together' when introducing austerity when of course it only affected the poorest. If people won't become vegetarians ban meat – watch how quickly supermarkets and food manufacturers will secure meat-free alternatives. If people won't stop eating fish ban it. Once the environment has healed we can reconsider these things, but I'm sure future humanity will look at us with disgust that we ever butchered trillions of animals for food. And I say this as somebody who has meat with every meal! If it saves the planet, and I hear enough vegans shouting that it does ('I'M A VEGAN BECAUSE I LIKE TO DO MY BIT FOR THE ENVIRONMENT – BUT I DON'T GO ON ABOUT IT!'), then we need to do it. Give and take – we all agree to lose, some more than others – I'm looking at you the 1%, and in return we commit to saving mankind's future.

I don't know about you but the scariest movies I see are the world extinction ones – *Armageddon, Deep Impact, 2012* etc. I know I won't live forever but the thought of the world dying, mankind dying, leaves me cold. (What will we watch from heaven? Repeats for eternity? It'll be like being stuck on the Beeb forever.) We all have so much potential if only we could learn to share.

Just a very quick note on religion – it's a book in its own right – but it's funny how nobody has yet commercialised the afterlife. Religions still champion that we will all live happy lives forever in heaven with loved ones with no hunger, no sadness, no suffering. Why isn't it like that on Earth then? People will fight and die for a religion and the sweet eternity awaiting them, yet they won't get off their ass to fight for it here. Look around – this planet is more beautiful than any God could design in heaven. It features absolute paradise in every direction and we have almost destroyed it. Why won't heaven be similar? Why won't the greedy people destroying this world, those for whom too much is never enough, not destroy heaven? Seriously, I'd love to know people's thoughts (and yes, of course I realise people have commercialised heaven whilst on Earth – it's called religion and it's the ultimate life insurance policy! I'm curious as to know why heaven will be different). I hate to channel Belinda Carlisle but 'ooh, Heaven is a place on Earth'. We've got to make it so, for everybody. It's probably all we're going to get for eternity. Religion enables the status quo with stupid messages like 'the meek shall inherit the earth', as we forgive the sins of the greedy. No more – Earth is heaven for some and hell for others. Let's even it up.

Law & Order

A slight deviation from the environment but how else can we improve society and ordinary people's quality of life? Their local environment. An obvious place for me to start is law and order. It's not that crime is out of control, but it is clearly getting worse. The murder rate in London is the highest it has been for a long time. How should we deal with crime? How should we deal with punishment and rehabilitation?

'We lost the war on drugs. Let's Party!' This is a slogan on a T-shirt worn by my friend who is a teacher. He gets high, baked, mashed, smashed, caned on everything. But not when it's a school night. Because he is a responsible member of society. His biggest failings, as with most recreational drug users, come when using that societally acceptable narcotic – alcohol. The tax man's drug of choice, and maybe mix it up with a fag or two as long as you put in more than you take out by way of the NHS. Ask any recreational drug user and the real pollutant to society is booze. Yes, there are drugs that are dangerous, addictive etc. but so is booze and that is what has turned every town or city centre into a no-go area for anybody who is not tanked up enough to consider a night out in such an environment as fun.

Anyway, back to drugs. It's a fool's errand for the police, because you can never beat people's desire to want to get high. I remember as a kid when you had Zammo on *Grange Hill* ('Just say no') and this idea of pushers at the school gates. In my experience it's been the users battling their way to the dealers. Every dealer I've ever known has tried to keep a low profile and only deal to contacts of contacts. People want to get off their nut and whilst booze helps, it should be understood that it's a diabolical drug if you look at the buzz you get for the cost and the physical damage. And cost to relationships.

A quick starting point if I may – you may be reading this and saying – 'I don't need to get high. I don't even drink. What's this fool on about?' Bully for you, but your life may not be full of stress, trapped in a crappy urban environment with pressures of work and family dragging you down. I accept I can get dopamine by going fell walking but I don't live near no fells and it takes hours to get there from Grays. And even if you do, it's not social. You'll never get your mates to go. If I want to get high naturally it will require a change of lifestyle that I simply can't afford in either time or money or friends. If I want to visit unnatural highs on a Friday and Saturday I can do it for a few quid in chemical form. This can be legal (lots of booze) or illegal (recreational drug of choice). My point is – fighting a losing war on narcotics consumption is foolish from a societal and economic point of view. Let's accept we are all different and whilst some of us can get through life with *Strictly Come Dancing* on a Saturday night, some of us want to get off our nuts to relax. Look at how society has responded to a war of attrition against smoking. Can't smoke indoors, can't smoke outside, but you can buy fags with pictures of wonky lungs on them telling you they will cause erectile dysfunction. OK– you win. I'm now almost out. And, being out of a heavy drinking and smoking scene, you know I am now less inclined to want to get high on gear. Have I beaten my demons? Maybe, or just gotten older, but people are smoking less despite nothing having fundamentally changed (other than less disposable income – perhaps there is a link! Maybe austerity did work out).

How do we do the same for drugs? Well for starters you don't decriminalise. Decriminalising keeps the wealth in the hands of the bad guys and simply legitimises them. Think of Las Vegas and gambling. What society needs to do is legalise it and police it like cigarettes and alcohol. Want to get high at the weekend? Rather than your kids going to see a dealer who may require favours for gear of poor quality (what is the cutting agent being used exactly?) it will be manufactured on licence by organisations with transparent quality control and hopefully product liability insurance. Tax it, control it. Stop people having to go to an underbelly of society that most of us don't want to go near. I hate big business with a passion but I would rather have my day in court with them than arguing with dealers, or worse getting caught between rival gangs in London (with London style crime spreading rapidly into Essex and other home counties).

The war on drugs has simply created Al Capone style gangs on a global scale with commensurate global wealth. We've seen countries ravaged by the cost of the need of Western politicians to act like puritanical, despite the fact we now have a third of the government coughing up to partaking themselves. For goodness sake when the PM has been strongly rumoured to do the odd line I really think it is time to consider that maybe getting buzzed isn't a reflection of any kind of moral failure. It just reflects a need for a slightly more specialist cup of coffee or whisky.

Slight tangent - I've often wondered whether societies have criminalised drugs to keep the working classes fighting amongst themselves. Rather than recognise the evil of big business and political corruption we have been distracted by concerns over who is going to nick our car or our mobile. The flip side is it provides black market employment in poor areas, also diverting people from focusing on a lack of work in many poorer areas, areas often dominated by immigrant and ethnic communities. It's unlikely of course, but not beyond the realms of possibility.

Anyway – aside from my diatribe – where do we go from here? Imagine a world of legal drugs. Everything scrutinised and taxed. Health or addiction problems – see your doctor. Support groups and addiction groups with no stigma – financed by the manufacturers. You probably imagine absolute carnage of drug fuelled chaos, but remember we see that every weekend through alcohol and society survives. Indeed, aside from the violence caused by too much alcohol there is no associated violence from the pushers or dealers. Kids from Heineken ain't stabbing those from SAB Miller. The only people who will lose from legalised drugs are the criminals themselves. Not just those involved in drugs but those serious people involved in the supply chain. Think how drugs get to the UK. It requires border guards and people in authority to look the other way. Now, picture yourself as a customs official on the Turkish/Iranian border. You're offered half a years' salary a month to look the other way on certain shipments making their way through. Drugs destined for Western Europe. 'Not my problem if those idiots want to grow poppies in their arms'. Indeed not. However, what happens after a year when you are offered two years' salary to properly look the other way? – this is when it could be people, or terrorism. You are now in a problem position. You don't want to be a part of this but what do you do? You can't cough to the authorities now, you're complicit. You just have to keep your eyes shut and pray for the best knowing you have blood on your hands but you're trapped. The war on drugs enables these supply chains to exist. My town Grays recently experienced the tragic case of Vietnamese migrants being discovered frozen in a reefer container. How did they get through without such supply chains existing? People smuggling is not regular enough to maintain these chains. Drugs is the bread and butter that sets these networks up and maintains them. People smuggling is a value added service provided to other criminals.

As much as we all wish people didn't need to get high, we have to recognise that they do. Prohibition of alcohol created organised crime networks that still linger in the US today. Prohibition of drugs will create criminals that will linger for centuries unless we are grown up enough to say – demand and supply – which side do we want the good guys to control? We've never been able to police prostitution because there is a demand and a supply. It is a shame but it's the real world. Let's bring it into the light and protect everybody. Drugs is the same. All the support is currently in place for booze and fags. We've reduced smoking and drinking by changing behaviour and education. We can do the same with drugs. And if people think it will be chaos, it won't. I can get off my nut on booze seven nights a week. Hell, Tesco's deliver the UK's drug of choice to your door. I don't get sozzled every night. Why not? Because I have a job, a family, responsibilities. I can get gear of all sorts from mates within forty- eight hours, and probably less in a push. I don't and why not? Because I have a job, a family, responsibilities and recognise the health implications of ingesting something completely unknown into my body. In the same way as considering the environment we have to look at the big picture. Statistically there are certain people whose lives have been harmed, most often by others, who need to self-medicate. It's tragic but it's the way of the world – let's help them. It doesn't matter what is legal and what's not, the ability to blur reality is a means to numb the pain. Addiction will always happen, but if we accept that there are understandable reasons for it, we become grown up enough to move past the moral right/wrong argument and look at how to protect society as a whole. Make it all legal, via heavily regulated, tax paying suppliers who finance the societal costs of the damage their drug does and educate the users on the damage. Stop the supply chains who are destroying transit countries and establishing crime at all levels of those societies. Stop the disorganised, dangerous crime at street level, and organised crime higher up.

Prohibition doesn't work. If you prohibited marbles there would be kids up and down the country playing marbles in school, at bus stops, in shopping centres. There would be dealers and there would be stabbings and shootings as people try to make a turn on it. There would be urban music artists rolling marbles in videos. It sounds hilarious but think it through. That is the price of prohibition. Worst of all you turn something frankly pretty farcical (middle-age cabinet ministers doing cocaine) into something rebellious and romantic in the eyes of some youth. People talk about cannabis being a gateway drug but it's prohibition that's the gateway. You don't see kids down the park with decanters of port even though it's legally available. You probably won't see as much legal drug consumption once the legalisation has calmed down as people won't want to be doing the same narcotics as their old dears. Remember the same drugs are still being used as the UK high streets of thirty years ago. Or the social elite of fifty-plus years ago. Once it's no longer legal it will be seen for what it is. It's not hip, it's not cool – it will reduce quickly.

We also have situations where the black market competition has resulted in stronger and more harmful forms of narcotic. The THB factor within cannabis is reckoned to have increased significantly over the years, resulting in increased rates of psychosis amongst users. This would be prevented in a controlled system. Ah, but a black market would then exist for the enhanced gear. Perhaps, but then would a user really want to move away from the high street and its controls to the back street and its risks? I once bought a pack of fags from a geezer in a pub on the promise they were smuggled and so really cheap. One fag down and I dread to think what it was, but it was lung cancer right there. Never again.

If we stop the nonsense of a war on drugs we can use all of that resource to fighting addictions and the damage they cause. I've seen loved ones' lives ruined and finished because of alcohol. I've seen early deaths of loved ones caused by smoking. I've seen the innocent families of gamblers have

117

their lives destroyed because of a family member's addiction. All of these are legal – so we either fight these as well (like King Knut it is futile and stupid to fight the tide of people's behaviour) or we apply the same logic to all narcotics. My only concern on this is how hundreds of thousands of UK citizens will replace their earnings if the black market was to disappear.

You are probably worried about the power of big business and their lobbyists. I agree, but remember – no more gaming of the system. The people and their honest representatives will determine an acceptable amount of profit for the manufacturers and sellers of drugs. Let's learn from cigarettes the correct way to reduce societal risk – ban advertising, add heavily regulated warnings of health concerns, push it to the margins of acceptable society so that it is uncool rather than prohibited and cool.

The downsides of drugs already exist within society – crime, violence and addiction. Can it really get any worse? I would also add that alternative drug culture to alcohol may be just what our high streets and stretched NHS require. Chilled coffee shops (again, heavily regulated) may be just what we've been looking for. We didn't get the continental café culture we were hoping for by extending licencing hours – perhaps diluting alcohol's grip on our society may benefit us all?

Violence

I was shocked to read an article recently featuring Cressida Dick, the current head of the Met, pleading for a prison sentence for those who attack the police on two separate occasions. This really shocked me. There really can be no excuse for violence in our society, and even less against those persons putting their lives on the line to police it. Of course the police make mistakes, and their punishment should reflect their greater responsibility, but similarly violence has to stop. If this is how the police are supported when they are attacked it makes you wonder what level of support the ordinary citizen could expect to receive from the justice system.

Violence in society has to stop. How to stop it? Well, there are obvious structural issues surrounding economic inequality, but even then that doesn't fully explain it away. Read any newspaper and the perpetrators of violence you see on a daily basis will more than likely have jobs. They are not desperate people. We're not talking about drug gangs and organised violence, but the day to day grind of road rage, pavement rage, parking rage, trolley rage, shopping rage. Unfortunately, we have allowed a culture of violence to grow, and it needs to be stopped.

When I was growing up there was always this image of the missus trying to hold back her fella with a cry of 'Leave it, Gal, 'e ain't worth it!', whereas nowadays you get the impression she'd be jumping up and down on the other person's head with the best of them. There seems to be no moment for pause.

I would suggest that any threat of violence, or minor act of violence, be dealt with through an inconvenience custody. If the average annual holiday entitlement is five weeks, then any conflict scenario and you are inside for five weeks – not prison, that would still be there if deemed appropriate, but essentially a souped-up budget hotel. There can be no excuse for violent acts, or threats of violence, to only receive fines or community service as a punishment. That simply emboldens the perpetrator and encourages others around them. Low level scuffle – five weeks in. You miss your holidays, but you keep your job. You get to think seriously about what you did and why. You get to assess your life without losing it all. Such places could have training courses – financial planning, anger management, yoga, meditation, exercise, art, nutrition. It is the opportunity to turn somebody's life around without denying them a future. Three years clean and the record is wiped. No mobile phones, no television, guidance books only. Essentially five weeks of self-help and opportunity for improvement. Take the piss and you're going to be doing proper time.

Prison is not the answer because it generally creates a path of reoffending as opposed to rehabilitation. If you make somebody into a criminal (i.e. criminal record limiting life opportunities) you are still left with a criminal in society at the end of the custodial sentence. Yet, at the same time, we can't have people getting away with threats or acts of violence – there has to be a strict liability on this. A few years in to this and the mind-set of 'leave it, they're not worth it' will come back.

Does anybody know why UK prisons don't block mobile phone signals? Surely if phones are being smuggled, and those phones enable criminal activities to be maintained by prisoners, the obvious solution is to kill the network.

Also – no excuses for foreign criminals. We have enough of our own scumbags, thank you. Foreigner – deported. I would expect nothing less of other countries against a British thug – why should we treat foreigners more favourably? As mentioned in the section on immigration, it needs to be seen as a contract of employment. You mess up, you're sacked. Commit a crime – visa withdrawn.

Housing

Housing policy has been a disaster since the 80s when the decision was made to sell off council housing and deregulate the financial industry.

This process has enabled private persons to benefit from massive public subsidies whilst taking housing stock away from the nation and those who need it. In turn this has seen a massive rise in house prices as demand outstrips supply for housing, combined with that increased demand fuelling a buy to let boom for the last two decades.

As noted above we need to find a way to spread work beyond major cities – hopefully that would see a flattening of house prices across the country, as people are more able to take advantage of working more remotely. However, that in itself is not going to be enough whilst population increases faster than number of properties. The solution – smaller properties. Now, hear me out. Before the obvious criticism of shoddy new builds is thrown at me, I am not proposing smaller new builds for families or younger people. I think the solution is new builds for older people, but not old-folks' homes. If part of the blockage for housing is older, single persons still living in family homes – understandably reluctant to move into retirement homes, rather than making crappy new homes, why don't we build edge of town developments for older persons?

Small, single bedroomed properties (ideally from environmentally friendly prefabs), with a single drive and small, manageable gardens. And unlike building for an unknown future population, where both planners and developers are always playing catch up, pensioners are a known quantity. The numbers can be planned for.

Another aim should be to redevelop our crap towns. Unsurprisingly Grays town centre is on the list of 100 desperate high streets to receive funding from Boris Johnson's revitalisation plan. But why can't we look to target run-down towns for a makeover? In the same way that cities all over the world bid for Olympics host city status, why can't we have British towns bidding to be champions every four years? The winner could have special tax status for companies, residents and employees, creating a boom town. In exchange that town would have to commit to redevelopment – public transport, housing, education, libraries, theatres, hospitals. The existing population get the benefits of low tax rates and high government spending in exchange for allowing a mass, planned development. Perhaps in the way that towns have competed for City status or City of Culture in the past?

We have to stop people owning more than one property. If, as a society, we want to push home ownership for all, we can't have persons having multiple properties. We need a licencing system whereby each local authority is required to grant out licences for renting and these can only be obtained by publicly listed companies who have been through a robust tender process. The reason for the publicly listed element is that everybody in society can elect to still partake in property as an investment, but at least controls would be within the hands of the authorities. It is wrong on so many levels that people can have numerous properties whilst others have none. If people have excess wealth they buy a bigger single property, not four properties. If people have excess wealth they invest it in the real economy.

Thanks

Thanks for reading. Whether you agree or not with the thoughts in this piece I hope you will have a clearer understanding of the considerations of many Brexit voters. Brexit is a result of the repeated failure of the British political classes to sufficiently address the real-life issues affecting the majority of the UK population, combined with a feeling of loss of control due to the opaque nature of politics in Brussels.

Whether the future is within the EU or not, there are issues that must be addressed if we are not to risk an even greater splintering of society, which potentially risks our stability. For me, Brexit is the pained birth of a new type of society. The UK has led the world for hundreds of years – trade, industry, politics, economics, democracy, culture. Where this country leads the world has followed. Environmental destruction is upon mankind. A new form of society needs to be engineered where consumption is rejected for all but the essentials. A new focus needs to be brought on quality of life, and the foundation for this needs to be greater distribution of wealth. No more can mankind's destiny be driven by the few who are lucky enough to have the wealth to overly exert their influence.

Let every voice be heard, and whilst we can never guarantee equality in outcome, let's agree that each person should have equality of influence. Let's stop the system being gamed.

www.ingramcontent.com/pod-product-compliance
Lightning Source LLC
Chambersburg PA
CBHW060407290526
45791CB00002B/644